By Harold H. Bloomfield, M.D.

TM: Discovering Inner Energy and Overcoming Stress (with Michael P. Cain, Dennis T. Jaffe, and Robert B. Kory)
Happiness (with Robert B. Kory)
How to Survive the Loss of a Love (with Melba Colgrove, Ph.D., and Peter McWilliams)
The Holistic Way to Health and Happiness (with Robert B. Kory)
How to Enjoy the Love of Your Life
Inner Joy (with Robert B. Kory)
Making Peace with Your Parents (with Leonard Felder, Ph.D.)

By Leonard Felder, Ph.D.

Learning to Love Forever (with Adelaide Bry)
Making Peace with Your Parents (with Harold H. Bloomfield, M.D.)

MAKING PEACE
WITH YOUR
PARENTS

MAKING PEACE WITH YOUR PARENTS

Harold H. Bloomfield, M.D.

with Leonard Felder, Ph.D.

Random House   New York

Inquiries about the content of this book should be addressed to
Harold H. Bloomfield, M.D., 1011 Camino Del Mar, Del Mar,
California 92014

Grateful acknowledgment is made to Merriam-Webster, Inc.,
for permission to reprint an entry from *Webster's New
Collegiate Dictionary*, © 1981 by Merriam-Webster, Inc.,
publisher of the Merriam-Webster Dictionaries.

Library of Congress Cataloging in Publication Data

Bloomfield, Harold H., 1944–
Making peace with your parents.

1. Parent and child. 2. Adult children—Family
relationships. 3. Parents. 4. Parents, Aged. 5. Family.
6. Interpersonal relations. I. Felder, Leonard.
II. Title.
HQ755.85.B58   1983   306.8'74   83–42771
ISBN 0-394-53414-X

Manufactured in the United States of America
24689753

For my dearly beloved wife, Sirah,
newborn daughter, Shazara,
mother, Fridl, departed father, Max, and sister, Nora,
and to children and parents everywhere who want to
share more peace and love.

ACKNOWLEDGMENTS

I wish to thank all from whom I have drawn ideas and inspiration, especially Werner Erhard, Elisabeth Kübler-Ross, Arnold Lazarus, Maharishi Mahesh Yogi, Abraham Maslow, Carl Rogers and my clients at the North County Holistic Health Center in Del Mar, California.

Appreciation is given to Mary Ellen Bayer, Truen Bergen, Adelaide Bry, Terry Cole-Whittaker, Carolyn Crowne, Lyn Davis, Ken and Karen Druck, Warren Farrell, Jan Fillmore, Mike and Donna Fletcher, Robert Kory, Linda Lawson and Tracy Weston, Patricia McDonough, Barnett Meltzer, Kenneth Miller, Barbara Nussbaum, Al Pesso, Jennifer Polito, Peter Reiss, Ali and Sybil Rubottom, Janice and Craig Ruff, Linda Seger, Gay Swenson, and Chris and Carolyn Tesari.

For their guidance and suggestions I especially acknowledge William and Anita Fitelson, Marc Jaffe and Lucy Kroll. Special thanks to Charlotte Mayerson for her intelligence, good taste and warm friendship in editing this book.

Leonard would like to thank Linda Schorin, Martin and Ena Felder, Jesse Bayer and Helen Rothenberg Felder for their support and encouragement.

I would like to express my love and deep appreciation to my wife, Sirah Vettese, for her devotion, contributions to the book, and assisting me in making peace with my parents.

Contents

Author's Note

To protect confidentiality, the names and identifying details in the case histories reported within the book have been changed. Any resemblance to persons living or dead is purely coincidental. Anyone with a history of psychiatric disorder, or who feels emotionally unstable, or who is taking major tranquilizers or antidepressant medication, should not do the exercises in this book without first consulting a qualified mental-health professional.

MAKING PEACE
WITH YOUR
PARENTS

1

A Personal Challenge

In the middle of a nationwide promotional tour for one of my books in the fall of 1978, I received a long-distance call from my mother. She was crying as she said, "You've got to come home. Your father's in the hospital. He's having emergency surgery for cancer."

I caught the next plane to New York. The thought that my father might die terrified me not only because of how much I loved him but because he and I had so much unfinished business to take care of. He had always been my father, but I felt that I barely knew him as a person. I was filled with guilt that on some level it was my fault he had developed cancer; that if I had not stayed away from my parents so much, maybe I could have done more for him.

Up until that phone call, I had thought that I had my relationship with my parents "handled." Living more than three thousand miles away from them, I would join my mother and father for an occasional lunch or dinner when a lecture, book tour or business matter brought me back to New York. I would make sure to limit the reunions to an hour or two. By holding a tight lid on my conflicting feelings for my parents, I had always managed to avoid a direct confrontation during our strained conversations. While hardly enjoying the visits or our routine once-a-week phone calls, all of us nevertheless kept up the appearance of a caring family.

For most of my life, I had thought of my father as a victim and had felt sorry for the many frustrations he suffered. He often complained that his work didn't satisfy or adequately reward him. At home, most of the time my parents either argued or kept a hostile silence; the tension was such that I remember thinking as a child, "God, just let me survive now and I'll heal later." While I loved my father, I also resented him for never breaking out of his rut. After struggling for his entire life, he had reached the age of sixty-five to face a hopeless decision—work until he dropped dead or retire to spend twenty-four hours a day with my mother.

On the plane during the flight to New York to my father's hospital bed, I sensed that you don't get to heaven alone—you take your family with you. I realized that I had the opportunity to make this visit different from all the others. Even though I knew I could try to fake my way through it by bringing my father flowers while still holding all my feelings inside, I made up my mind that I was going to reestablish closeness with each of my parents. Keeping them at arm's length was no longer what I wanted. After years of resenting my obligatory reunions with my parents and blaming them for how unenjoyable it all was, this time I would make myself responsible for what I got out of the visit. I had never before viewed my training in medical school, psychiatry and human-potential seminars as a vehicle for relating to my own parents, yet it was clear that God or nature was saying, "O.K., Bloomfield, let's see how much you've really learned."

The Two-hundredth Hug

My father's skin was jaundiced as he lay hooked up to monitors and intravenous tubes in the intensive care unit of the hospital. Normally a well-built man, he had lost more than thirty pounds.

My father's illness had been diagnosed as cancer of the pancreas, one of the most malignant forms of the disease. The doctors were doing what they could but told us that he had only three to six months to live. Cancer of the pancreas does not lend itself to radiation therapy or chemotherapy, so they could offer little hope.

A few days later, when my father was sitting up in bed, I approached him and said, "Dad, I really feel for what's happened to you. It's helped me to look at the ways I've kept my distance and to feel how much I really love you." I leaned over and started to give him a hug, but his shoulders and arms tensed up.

"C'mon, Dad, I really want to give you a hug."

For a moment he looked shocked. Showing affection was not our usual way of relating. I asked him to sit up some more so I could get my arms around him. Then I tried again. This time, however, he was even more tense. I could feel the resentment starting to build inside me, and I was almost ready to say something like "I don't *need* this. If you want to leave me with the same coldness as always, go right ahead."

For years I had used every instance of my father's resistance and rigidness to blame him, to resent him and to say to myself, "See, he doesn't care." This time, however, I thought again and realized the hug was for *my* benefit as well as my father's. I wanted to express how much I cared for him no matter how hard it was for him to let me in. My father had always been very Germanic and duty-oriented; in his childhood his parents must have taught him how to shut off his feelings in order to be a man.

Letting go of my long-held desire to blame him for our distance, I was actually looking forward to the challenge of giving him more love. I said, "C'mon, Dad, put your arms around me."

I leaned up close to him at the edge of the bed with his arms around me. "Now squeeze. That's it. Now again, squeeze. Very good!"

In a sense I was showing my father how to hug, and as he squeezed, something happened. For an instant, a feeling of "I love you" sneaked through. Where for years our greeting had been a cold and formal handshake that said "Hi, how are you?" now both he and I waited for that momentary closeness to happen again. Yet just at the moment when he would begin to enjoy the feelings of love, something would tighten in his upper torso and our hug would become awkward and strange. It took months before his rigidness gave way and he was able to let the emotions inside him pass through his arms to encircle me.

It was up to me to be the source of many, many hugs before my father initiated a hug on his own. I was not blaming him; after all, he was changing the habits of an entire lifetime—and that takes time. I knew we were succeeding because more and more we were relating out of care and affection. Around the two-hundredth hug, he spontaneously said out loud, for the first time I could ever recall, "I love you."

A Time for Healing

My father's cancer became an opportunity for growth and change within my family. I found myself practicing the compassion and understanding I had been teaching my patients. With my assistance, my mother and father began to work out some of the buried resentments and emotional distance that had long accumulated between them. My older sister and I joined them in family meetings during which we were able to share our feelings more honestly and lovingly than ever before.

Ever since I had studied to become a teacher of Transcendental Meditation (TM), my father had dismissed my strong interest in meditation as "weird" and "impractical." Now, as though he had suddenly heard my point of view for the first time, he enrolled in the basic TM course and was soon meditating twice a day. I also taught him the visualization technique prescribed by Dr. Simonton,* during which my father would picture his white cells going to and gobbling up the cancer cells, apparently mobilizing his body's defenses against the disease. In addition to the stress reduction and visualization techniques, my father began to improve his condition through diet, physical exercise and planning trips with my mother.

*For more on visualization as an adjunct to cancer therapy, see Carl Simonton et al., *Getting Well Again: A Step-by-Step Self-Help Guide to Overcoming Cancer for Patients and Their Families* (Los Angeles: Tarcher, 1978).

The healing and growth in my family meant that each of us released a whole backlog of resentments, suppressed anger and love. As a result, my father no longer remained stuck in the role of victim or martyr. Instead of blaming his cancer on my mother by saying, as had been his custom, "You did it to me . . . it's your fault," he powerfully regained his will to live. He and my mother began to enjoy life more than they had in years.

When my parents came to my home near San Diego for three incredible weeks with my wife-to-be, Sirah, and me, I felt that my father was my oldest and dearest friend. Sirah and I were giving him lots of love and he was responding with lots of love for her and me. The tension was gone; our time together was very loving and close. We each knew it would be his last time at my home, yet we felt a sense of tremendous gratitude. The doctors had predicted three to six months; my father had survived the cancer for over *four high-quality years.*

One night after we took my parents out for dinner, my father sat in my hot tub as I massaged his neck and shoulders. With the attention I gave his muscles, he was absolutely melting. We no longer had our defenses up toward each other and for a time we both had the sense that we were one.

My parents, Sirah and I had finally become the close-knit family we had always pretended to be. After we celebrated a very special Father's Day, my parents went back to New York, where my father died a few weeks later. His life complete, his relationships with his wife and children having come full circle, he died in a state of grace.

Those four years of peace with my parents made a tremendous difference in my life. Seeing the two of them having a good relationship freed me to stop perceiving marriage as a

prison. With a new and exciting model of love and commitment in my mind, I was able to break through my fears of
and resistance to marriage. From healing my resentments
and sharing more love with my parents, I also gained inner
peace.

The Price We Pay

If I had never found out what it was like to really feel my
parents' love, I would have missed a tremendous opportunity. I decided to write *Making Peace with Your Parents*
because I understood the harmful price we each pay by
having an incomplete and strained relationship with our parents. No matter how we try to rationalize our distance and
resentments, or think that we have the relationship "handled," there are emotional wounds and even health burdens
that we suffer from the unfinished business with our parents.

For the longest time, I thought that keeping up my defenses was the only way to relate to my parents. When they
would offer unsolicited advice during our phone conversations, I would simply pretend to listen. When I visited them,
I told myself that all I could hope for was to make the best
of a difficult situation. Even though I functioned as a competent adult in other areas of my life, when I encountered my
mother and father I still had the point of view of a helpless
and victimized child. I treated the relationship as their responsibility, not mine.

Underneath the protective armor I wore whenever I faced
my parents, there were conflicting feelings tugging at me. I
loved my parents and at the same time couldn't stand them.
I felt guilty while I dreaded that I might become like them

or that my love relationships would remind me of their embittered marriage.

The worst part was our inability to communicate. We pretended we were devoted to one another, yet we could not show or feel that emotion because of hidden resentments. It was unacceptable to express anger in my family and much too risky to be affectionate or loving. All those years the love between us was unspoken and often unnoticed. Then my father got cancer and it was almost too late.

As a psychiatrist and the co-director of a health center, I see countless instances in which people have emotional, relationship, career and even physical problems in their day-to-day lives that can be understood and alleviated only by tracing back more deeply to their unresolved conflicts with their parents. Many of the here-and-now conflicts people have with their spouses, lovers, ex-lovers, bosses, partners or children are in part emotional reenactments of suppressed feelings stored from incidents that happened when they were children. The same unresolved conflicts they had with their parents always seem to "mysteriously" reappear to affect their adult relationships.

For instance, Karl is a patient of mine who came to our clinic complaining of severe backaches. Sometimes he would be flat on his back for a week after his muscles went into spasm. Even though Karl had not spoken to his father in more than ten years, we quickly discovered that his angry outbursts directed toward his wife, teenage sons and boss could be traced back to unresolved feelings of anger and frustration that he never expressed to his harsh disciplinarian father. The deep resentments Karl had been harboring for years contributed to both the physical and interpersonal conflicts he was having.

In a similar fashion, Deborah came to the clinic to work out her problems with men. She complained that "I always find I am attracted to the kind of guys I can't trust." Divorced once and the mother of a ten-year-old daughter, Deborah wanted to find out how to break her pattern of short-lived, frustrating relationships.

When I asked her what her parents' relationship was like, Deborah described how her mother, an intelligent woman who had dropped out of a top college to get married, sacrificed herself for a man who "never lived up to his potential." When Deborah first began to go out with boys in high school, her mother warned her, "Don't settle for someone like your father." Now Deborah realized how much the conflict between her mother and father was still affecting her relationships with men.

Regardless of status or income, no one seems to be immune to the complex and harmful effects of an unresolved conflict with one's parents. One of my closest friends is a well-known forty-eight-year-old physician who lives in Minnesota. Hard-working, innovative, fun-loving and a family man with a wife and four grown children, he has always impressed me with his vitality. Yet the last time he visited me, when we were showering after a game of basketball, I noticed a huge outbreak of eczema (an irritating skin ailment) all over his back and shoulders.

I asked my friend, "How did you get that?"

Somewhat embarrassed, he laughed and said, "My mother just came to visit for two weeks. I get this same flare-up every time she comes to Minneapolis."

In spite of his seeming to "have it all together," this eminent physician had broken out in an irritating rash, apparently from unresolved tensions with his mother. When I told him about *Making Peace with Your Parents,* he smiled and said, "I'll take two copies and call you in the morning!"

Then his expression became serious, as he admitted, "It's funny about parents. I've been trying to ignore my mixed feelings about my mother for years." Pointing to the eczema sores on his back, he added, "But it's hard to ignore this kind of physical reaction."

Why Wait?

You do not have to wait for a crisis in which you are sick or one of your parents is dying to make peace with your mother and father. There are compelling reasons to start right now. Whether you are twelve or eighty-two, you may be carrying around many of the pressures and unresolved conflicts of that most fundamental relationship, the one you have (or had) with your parents. These heavily charged, suppressed emotions play an important role in determining your day-to-day health and happiness.

In order to assess the extent to which you can benefit from *Making Peace with Your Parents,* consider the following questions:

1. Are you free of regrets and resentments from your childhood?

2. Do you feel relaxed and at your best when you get together with your parents?

3. Are you able to recognize when you are angry in the present as a result of a resentment or unresolved hurt from your childhood?

4. Can you trust your parents and confide in them?

5. Do you enjoy phone calls with your parents?

6. Are you confident about your ability and desire to be a good parent?

7. Are you able to forgive your parents without trying to change them?

8. Do you feel comfortable taking care of your aging parent(s)?

9. Can you accept the reality of a parent dying?

10. Are you glad you had the parents you did?

11. Do you feel loved and accepted by your parents?

12. Have you come to grips with your mixed feelings about your parents' divorce?

13. Have you completed your resentments and regrets toward your parent who is no longer living?

For each time you were unable to give a quick and honest "Yes" response, there will be a portion of *Making Peace with Your Parents* to assist you. The book includes both the psychological insights and the practical strategies to help you understand your relationship with your parents, defuse the painful emotions you carry inside and rebuild a healthy relationship with your mother and father.

In addition to helping you make peace with your parents, the insights and exercises in this book address a number of other critical issues that are indirectly affected by your relationship with your parents. Having conflicting and unresolved feelings about them can affect your moment-to-moment health and well-being, your satisfaction with your career, work and leisure time, and your most significant emotional relationships. Every day of the year marriages and loving relationships break up in part because one or both partners are plagued by unresolved hurts and conflicts from their earlier relationships with their parents. As we have seen, running battles with ex-lovers, in-laws, bosses, children, relatives and friends tend to be emotional replays of earlier parental conflicts.

To begin to comprehend the extent to which your relationship with your parents affects your daily life and peace of mind, give an honest answer to each of the following:

1. Do you feel free of the expectations and obligations of others?

2. Can you make a mistake without excessive self-criticism?

3. Are you able to express anger effectively without turning it inward or reacting with blind rage?

4. Are you good at both nurturing yourself emotionally and supporting yourself materially?

5. Are you comfortable with your sexuality?

6. Do you work well with bosses, teachers, landlords and other authority figures?

7. Are you free from paralyzing fears of rejection, disapproval or abandonment?

8. Have you overcome your fears of being trapped by a committed love relationship or marriage?

9. Are you free from excessive striving and unrealistic expectations that make you a slave to your work?

10. Are you good at setting limits for people who impose upon you?

11. Do you and your spouse or lover work through your arguments without blaming or holding on to resentments?

12. Do you appreciate and love yourself fully?

13. Do you feel fulfilled by your current home environment and family life?

14. Do you enjoy being responsible for your own happiness, emotions and the quality of your life?

What to Expect

Making Peace with Your Parents is not an overnight cure-all. It is a compilation of the experiences and insights of patients and workshop participants over the past eleven years. Combining my own experiences in my family with the research of my colleagues, the case histories of my patients, the literature in the field, and recent breakthroughs in psychiatry, I have developed a series of easy-to-follow exercises and personal growth skills that you can use effectively *whether your parents are alive or have died.* Each of us carries inside the emotional memories from his or her childhood. This book will help you learn to rediscover your personal power to master those complex emotions and to create an adult life as loving, joyful and fulfilling as you desire.

The process of making peace with your parents will take persistence and creativity for maximum success. The cases and personal accounts within the book serve as realistic examples of the variety of ways patients have used these techniques, resulting in differing rates of personal growth and change. While names have been disguised to preserve confidentiality, these examples are typical of the rapidity with which change can occur if the intention is there. Many thousands of people have already made enormous strides in improving their health, happiness and love relationships using these insights and skills.

The key to personal growth is not only *awareness* but *behavior change.* As you read the discussions and exercises and put them into practice, you can expect to gain the following:

　　—A far more extensive understanding of the relationship you had with your parents in your childhood and adolescence. That includes problems and conflicts as well as deep feelings of love you may have long ago suppressed.

　　—The ability to heal your hidden resentments and emotional hurts. These exercises will help prevent past upsets from "mysteriously" reappearing in your current relationships.

　　—The understanding and insight necessary to forgive your parents and learn to enjoy them exactly the way they are. This does not mean forgetting or stuffing away your feelings. Rather, you will be shown how to work through your anger successfully and get beyond your judgments and expectations in order to rediscover your ability to love and be loved by your parents.

　　—Effective communication skills to help you break out of the frustrating rut you and your parents have fallen into. Learning to express anger and love effectively and constructively will help you not only with your parents but with all of your relationships.

　　—Special insights and techniques to deal with "difficult" parents, including those who are martyrs, dictators or unavailable. There will be a host of useful examples from patients who not only survived but grew from working through their differences within the most critical, neurotic or threatening family situations.

　　—A greater understanding of the ways in which you may have held back your sexual expression and joy as a result of your upbringing. You will be given effective skills for unraveling the complex double messages about sexuality

that parents give to their children, as well as techniques for throwing off parental inhibitions and increasing your sexual fulfillment.

—*An awareness of the ways in which marital conflicts are often related to unresolved issues with your parents.* There will be techniques to help you eliminate fears of intimacy and negative family patterns you may be bringing into your love relationships.

—*Ways to deal effectively with the death of a parent.* Losing a parent can be devastating and yet may signify a period of profound growth and maturation. You will discover how dealing with your parent's death can lead from crisis to personal breakthrough.

—*Self-parenting skills through which you can become a more nurturing and loving person for yourself and your children.* Problems with our children are often related to problems we had with our parents. Specific strategies will help you become more of the mother or father you wanted to be.

To make peace with your parents, you may have to give up a lot. You may have to give up your resentments, your anger, your annoyance, your desire to punish and your need to blame. You may have to give up resisting your parents and be prepared even for times when it appears that they win and you lose. You may have to learn to admire and respect a parent for whom you may now feel a degree of contempt or hate. Indeed, you may need to learn to accept your parents exactly the way they are rather than the way you think they should be.

Why bother, or who cares, you might say? It is not primarily for your parents, but for *you.* Your peace of mind, your love and work relationships, and your moment-to-moment aliveness may be at stake. The means for making a shift in your relationship with your parents—and primarily in yourself—are now available to you. Making peace with your parents is a personal challenge that will bring you enormous and lasting satisfaction.

2

From Resentment to Forgiveness

As a psychiatrist and personal-growth seminar leader, I have heard thousands of accounts of bitter conflicts between individuals and their parents. Yet in every instance, underneath the anger and resentment, one central truth is clear: *We each have a deep desire to love and be loved by our parents.* We want to let go of the anger, hostility and bitterness that keep us separate and unable to communicate.

In order to clean up your relationship with your real-life parents, however, *you must first make peace with your inner parents*—the internalized messages, feelings and conflicts you carry around inside your head. Your mind is a storehouse for the painful memories and hidden resentments from your childhood—the things your parents did that deeply hurt you or made you feel that your physical or psychological survival was threatened. Until you begin to work through that emotional backlog of accumulated resentments, a satisfying and harmonious relationship with your mother and father is almost impossible. Instead of permitting you to love and enjoy your parents, the hidden resentments will force you to find every opportunity to feel victimized by their actions, to blame them and to repeatedly act out the old negative patterns that you resent. No matter how noble your intentions to love and be loved by your parents, the resentments you harbor will sooner or later get in the way.

How often have you said or felt one of the following about your parents?

"I try to be nice, but they do things just to upset me."

"They're completely set in their ways. I can't talk to them."

"Sure I love them, but at the same time they drive me crazy."

"They just can't accept that I'm different from who they thought I would be."

"All they want to talk about is the past, and they never stop reminding me about things I would rather forget."

Notice that each of these attitudes implies that the conflict with your parents is primarily *their* fault, *their* responsibility. It is as though you are a helpless victim waiting for *them* to change or apologize. Don't hold your breath! For as long as you wait for them to make the first move, you will continue to be plagued by the hidden resentments you carry inside. This is especially true for those whose parents have died. No matter how much you may want to believe that you no longer have to deal with a departed parent, the fact remains that your feelings for that parent are very much alive in your mind.

Hidden Resentments

A resentment is a feeling of hurt or anger because someone threatens your survival. By survival, I mean not just your physical existence but the emotional "survival" of your self-conception: your opinions, your feelings or the things you identify with your self. During your childhood there were times when your parents, for whatever reasons, made you feel belittled, ignored, abandoned, manipulated or in other ways psychologically attacked. We each have a backlog of these painful memories that restrict us and reduce our vitality. The question is what to do with them.

Unfortunately, resentments toward parents are never safely tucked away in the past. They are like tiny emotional abscesses—pockets of venomous feelings that never disappear. Most of the time your mind is oblivious to past resentments. Yet every once in a while the process that Freud described as "repression" breaks down. You might have a frightening or hostile dream. You might have an argument that arouses suppressed feelings of anger toward one or both of your parents. You might find that when you are ill and need others to care for you, old resentments and fears will suddenly reemerge. While the childhood incident with your parents may itself remain hidden in your subconscious, the associated venomous feeling will once again be experienced.

Since people and situations in your current life will in certain ways resemble people and situations from your past, you can expect that stressful memories will be continually reactivated. Whether these resemblances to your parents are accurate or not, past resentments can subconsciously exert total command over your present feelings, thoughts, attitudes and behavior. The psychological truth is that holding on to our past resentments toward parents robs us of our current peace of mind and our ability to experience satisfaction in our here-and-now relationships.

When your spouse or lover says something minor that happens to remind you of your parents' nagging, your angry and blame-filled emotional reaction surprises you with its intensity. When your boss or partner acts authoritatively, old resentments toward your parents can cause you to lash out inappropriately. When your children or someone else's children demand things you never got as a child, your resentments can inhibit your desire to willingly nurture their needs.

These hidden resentments have the power to make your life miserable and often do not disappear on their own. Every time past resentments get reactivated in the present, your mind and body are subjected to harmful physical and emotional symptoms of stress. Your thinking will be clouded, your muscles may become tense, your heart may race and your blood pressure may rise. While you will probably assume that your anxious feelings are directly caused by the current incident, in fact the stress-filled reaction relates back to unresolved conflicts with your parents.

This chapter will show you a number of successful techniques for making peace with your inner parents. As a result, you will be better able to understand and deal effectively with your feelings toward your actual parents (whether they are alive or not). In addition to healing your relationship with your mother and father, the chapter will show you how to stop taking out your parental resentments on your spouse or lover, boss or partner, children or siblings, as well as on yourself.

Sources of Hidden Resentments

Hurt feelings and unresolved conflicts can get "stuffed" into your subconscious for many years. As far as you can tell, they have disappeared; you may rarely, if ever, be aware of painful incidents or feelings from your childhood affecting your day-to-day experience. Eventually, however, the chronic stress of unresolved emotional hurts can contribute to serious health problems (such as cancer, ulcers, hypertension and heart disease), career and job conflicts, marital problems and reduced vitality.

You can assume that hidden resentments may be festering inside if you

—Feel like getting back at or telling off your boss.

—Sometimes lose your temper over a small matter and say things you later wish you hadn't said.

—Get bogged down in frequent fights, disagreements, struggles for control and feelings of distrust with your spouse or lover.

—Feel left out, overlooked, unappreciated or taken for granted at home or at work.

—Suffer from frequent headaches, neck aches, backaches, stomach aches or other bodily aches and pains.

—Have a weight problem or go on eating binges when you are emotionally upset.

—Dread having to call, write or visit your parents.

—Still compare yourself and compete with one of your brothers or sisters.

—Poke fun at or make spiteful comments about those you love.

—Frequently feel disappointed by or bitter about your family, work, the world, life, God, other people.

—Feel your parents never showed their love for you.

—Try to make others feel sorry for you.

—Feel like you are frequently holding back anger from your spouse, lover, family, friends or children.

—Feel restricted in expressing your love for your spouse and family.

Taking the Next Step

Once you become aware that you may be harboring hidden resentments, the next step is to work them through. But for many people that is easier said than done. For example, one of my clients, Judy, had known for years that she carried a number of resentments for her mother and older sister. Ever since she was young, Judy has had a weight problem. She also has a petite and attractive mother and a devastatingly beautiful older sister. When Judy was growing up, she always felt inferior and unattractive compared to them and carried these feelings with her as part of her adult self-image.

Judy commented during her first session at our clinic, "I won't have any problem trying to find my resentments. I just look in the mirror and compare myself with my mother and sister."

During college, Judy had blamed her roommates for her weight problem, claiming, "They ate junk food all the time. It was impossible to be around my roommates and not gain weight." After a ten-month crusade to change her roommates' eating habits, the end result was, according to Judy, "Three energetic roommates eating raw vegetables and sprout salads while I was still thirty pounds overweight."

Throughout her career as an advertising copywriter, Judy enrolled in one weight-reduction program after another. Some of these required great sacrifice and discipline. Judy would begin by following each technique religiously, but found that "even though they promised to help me control my appetite, I continued to binge whenever I was upset."

Sometimes Judy would feel depressed about her weight problem for weeks at a time. "Everyone said I had such a pretty face. I wanted to kill the next person who talked about my pretty face. My flabby body was my enemy—some days I felt so unattractive I couldn't go outside or be seen by anyone. More than a few times I called in sick and fell behind in my work."

Judy's preoccupation with her weight was her way of avoiding having to deal with buried resentments, which were triggering anxiety in the present. The variety of stimuli that could remind her of her resentments toward her mother and sister was endless. For example, any sort of rejection from a boyfriend, her boss or anyone else would trigger old feelings of insecurity and anger toward her mother and older sister.

When she first came to our clinic, Judy insisted that her problem was physiological—her appetite was hard to control. She discovered, however, after her first few sessions, that "blaming it on my body was a big lie. It's not like I ate because I was hungry. I overate to shut down all the uncomfortable feelings I had in my life. It was living hell to look in the mirror and feel so dissatisfied with myself."

Today Judy's stomach is flat, and she has maintained her normal weight of 120 pounds for over a year. She looks lighter not only physically but emotionally as well. The change came after she used exercises like those that follow to release and work through her backlog of resentments against her mother and older sister. "It was incredible how many times I'd stuffed away my anger. I finally discovered I don't have to be just like them in order to feel good about myself." For the first time in her life, Judy was able to fully implement a health and weight-reduction program.

Her case illustrates an important principle that many other clients have also discovered: *Until you begin to let go of your resentments and forgive yourself and your family, every other positive health strategy you use may be severely undermined.* Judy could not solve her weight problem without: first, forgiving herself for becoming overweight and loving herself exactly as she is; and second, forgiving her mother and older sister for being the people who they are.

The Benefits of Forgiveness

According to *Webster's New Collegiate Dictionary,* to forgive is "to cease to feel resentment against (an offender); to give up resentment of or claim to requital for (an insult); to grant relief from payment of (a debt)."

In other words, *to forgive is to let go.*

It is your personal decision—do you want to let go of your resentments or do you still want revenge? If you are out for revenge, all your energy is bound up with the parent you resent. If you choose to work through your resentment, the release and the relief can make you free again.

To forgive does not mean that you have to whitewash all the disputes and differences that exist between you and your parents. Nor does it mean you have to treat your parents as though they are saints. Very simply, *to forgive your parents allows you to change your relationship from one of resentment and distrust to one of love.* You can disagree with them and still love them deeply. You can express your feelings of anger or sadness and not feel alienated from them. You can respect and appreciate the differences, and yet learn from them.

When you are holding on to resentments, the past is a nightmare and the present is filled with possibilities for arousing your suppressed anger. When you forgive your parents, your emotions lighten up. You are no longer defending yourself and fearing that someone or something will trigger your old hurts. You have regained your capacity to feel more love, not only for your parents but for all the people in your life.

What You Resist Persists

Even if you agree with the importance of forgiveness, there may be a variety of reasons why you have been unable to completely forgive your parents. For some people, the inability to forgive goes hand in hand with a desire to feel sorry for themselves. Rather than giving up their resentments and moving on to better things, many people prefer to lament their failures with comments like

"Nobody ever loved me."
"I can never get what I want."
"If only my parents had been different."
"You don't know what it was like for me when I was a kid."

Still others fail to work through their resentments toward their parents because they insist, "I have no resentments against anyone. I'm a good person and I don't hold grudges." Most of us would like to think of ourselves as "nice" or "grown-up," but denying that we have resentments keeps us stuck in our misery. Instead of working through their un-resolved feelings, many "nice" people get headaches, neck pains, ulcers or skin rashes, or else their buried hurt seeps out in acerbic comments or bickering. Whenever you hold on to animosity, it is like ingesting small doses of poison. The more you try to deny your resentments, the more you are plagued by stress-related symptoms. Withheld bitterness may be the reason why your sleep is interrupted, why your dreams are upsetting you or why you have trouble falling asleep. Quite often, people who insist "I've already forgiven everyone" go through life feeling burdened, victimized or "burnt-out." Many people whose parent was unavailable because of a divorce, or whose parent died, pretend the feelings of bitter-ness have passed. In spite of their good intentions, they are doing themselves and their loved ones a great disservice.

Finally, there are some people who simply cannot or will not forgive their parents for incidents they remember so painfully. No matter how much they understand the dangers of carrying around old emotional hurts, they insist,

"I'd rather hate them than love them."
"I'll never forgive that S.O.B. for what he (or she) did."
"They were horrible and deserve to be punished."

What these people fail to realize is that by holding on to their resentments, they surrender control over their own emotional well-being to the person who hurt them in the first place. In other words, they give the resentment power—the more they resist letting go of the past, the more the resent-ment controls their attitudes and behavior. By carrying a chip on your shoulder, you may be sacrificing your health and happiness in the vain hope that your persecutor will see how "wronged" you are.

First and foremost, the reason to forgive is to regain your emotional freedom and peace of mind. When you are unable or unwilling to forgive your parents, a strange thing happens: the emotional upset invariably reappears in a different but equally upsetting present-day situation. Even though you may believe that ignoring or stuffing away your resentments will put an end to them, the "What You Resist Persists" phenomenon includes such seemingly mysterious reappearances as the following:

—You marry someone who later begins to resemble the parent you resent.

—You discover that you have started to act "just like" the parent you may hate.

—You start treating your spouse or lover the way your parents treated each other.

—You find yourself having the same career or money conflict your father or mother had.

—You find yourself reenacting the same illnesses, upsetting events or upheavals that one or both of your parents went through.

—You re-create in your adult life emotionally upsetting situations very similar to the unresolved incidents of your childhood (only the characters and settings have changed).

Suppressed Love

Even more troubling than the mysterious reappearance of long-suppressed hurts is that hidden resentments invariably lead to a suppressed experience of love and joy throughout your life. When you are fighting back painful memories, holding the lid on your anger or harboring old resentments, it can affect your current relationships in a variety of ways.

For instance, if you have unresolved hurts and resentments toward your parents, you may have made a subconscious decision that intimacy is dangerous, making you unable to be open and vulnerable in relationships. You may be unable to show affection for the people you care for, including your spouse or lover or your children. When you keep your intimate relationships at arm's length and need to stay in complete control in order to feel safe, you wind up alone and isolated.

Healing Your Resentments

Learning to forgive from the heart has been advocated by our greatest spiritual and religious teachers since the beginning of recorded history. Modern psychological research and practice have helped to make this process more understandable and more manageable. On the following pages, I will describe a number of exercises that have proven successful for thousands of clients and workshop participants who have moved from resentment to forgiveness.

Even though these exercises deal with painful childhood feelings and incidents, their function is *not* for you to dwell in an endless morass of old resentments. Rather, the intention of each exercise is quite the opposite—you will be given the opportunity to heal old wounds in order to *free more energy* for enjoying, understanding and loving.

The exercises can be used effectively whether your parents are alive or not. As I stated earlier, the first step in making peace with your parents is to make peace with your inner parents. The techniques *do not* require that you discuss your resentments or painful emotions with your actual parents. Rather, these tools are for your own psychological house-cleaning.

Set aside some time to do these exercises on your own or with a friend. Some people experience a tremendous release after one or two of the exercises; some need to do all five. Those burdened with heavy resentments need to use these techniques repeatedly over a number of weeks before they feel free of their resentments.

I. MAKING A LIST

Prepare a list of your resentments toward each of your parents. Each painful memory or hurt should be described as specifically as possible. Detail is extremely important. It is not helpful to write generalizations like "I hate my father." Instead, remember an incident, feeling or conflict that upset you and write it out exactly as it happened, including any relevant details.

For example, on the list for your mother, you might have statements like

"I resent that you slapped me at school in the first grade in front of my friends."

"I resent feeling like you never wanted me to be born."

"I resent how you make it seem like I'm to blame for your unhappiness."

For your father's list, some examples might include

"I resent that you wouldn't stop drinking even though you knew what it was doing to the rest of us."

"I resent that you used to hit me without giving me a chance to explain my side of the story."

"I resent that you still won't lift a finger for yourself, even though you know Mom isn't feeling well."

On a list for both of them, clients have written

"I resent that you got divorced."

"I resent that you're always trying to tell me how to spend my money."

"I resent that you can't be nicer to_____[your spouse] even though he [or she] has tried to win your love."

"I resent that you two won't stop fighting with each other."

"I resent that you always compared me to_____."

You do not have to remember every last one of your resentments. After a certain point, when you have filled up an entire page or more, you will have reached a critical mass. Rest a few moments and see if there are any other important hurts that you may have forgotten. Looking at both the past and present, don't hold back. After you have added these additional resentments to your list, stop to inhale and exhale deeply a few times. Let any feelings come up and do not be afraid to cry. The resentments have been stored inside for a long time; releasing them may bring up feelings of anger, hurt or loss.

Remember that your purpose in preparing a list of resentments is not to dredge up old hurts to punish yourself or your parents. You are healing your wounds from childhood for the purpose of restoring your full capacity for love and understanding. *Under no circumstances should these lists be shown to your parents.* Cleaning things up with your real-life parents needs to wait until later. (See Chapter Three.)

2. VISUALIZING YOUR PARENT

When you were a small child and your parents knowingly or unknowingly did things that you resented, you were unable to speak up for yourself. The hurt, more often than not, was stuffed into your reservoir of unacknowledged pain and you did your best to pretend that nothing was wrong. Now that you are an adult, you no longer have to pretend or feel victimized by your parents.

This exercise uses creative imagery to give you the opportunity to visualize your parents hearing you completely, acknowledging your pain fully and accepting your feelings. Regardless of how your actual parent would respond to your descriptions of your past hurts or whether or not your parent is still alive, in this exercise you will imagine him or her giving all the love, support and respect that you desire.

Begin by finding a comfortable spot in a private room. Unplug the phone and put a "Do Not Disturb" sign on the door so you will be undisturbed for at least thirty minutes. Then decide which parent to work with on this occasion. Take out your list of resentments toward that parent and slowly read it. After you are done, close your eyes and visualize yourself and your parent in an appropriate setting (e.g., the home you grew up in or perhaps the room you are in right now). If you find it difficult to visualize your parent, look at a photograph of him or her beforehand.

With your parent's image in mind, say in your own words, "Out of the love that I know deep down I have for you and out of the love that I know underneath it all you have for me, there are some things I need to clean up with you." Now proceed to let your inner parent know your feelings about the resentments on your list. It is not important to cover every last one. You may want to spend an entire session or two on one major traumatic event. Deal with whatever resentments come to mind.

As you are describing your resentments to your imagined parent, a number of feelings may come up. To get your anger, rage, hurt or sadness out of your system is the purpose of the exercise. Play-act, exaggerate your feelings, scream out loud —do anything to let your feelings go. Give yourself permission to act out your rage by having a pillow or mattress nearby to pound and physically release these feelings. In this exercise you are seeking to work through the negative aspects of your upbringing. Even the most ideal parents have some negative aspects to their parenting. Remember, however, that you are going to act out your violent feelings *only in this visualization exercise and not in real life.*

If you become distracted or feel emotionally blocked, bring yourself back to the task at hand. Remember that your intention is not to harm or disrespect your parents. Rather, you are using this imagery and letting your rage come out in order to release old hurts that are preventing you from making peace with your parents.

With each resentment, visualize your parent hearing you, acknowledging your hurt and understanding your feelings. Imagine your parent giving you complete permission to finally "let it out." Even if it is just in your imagination and could never happen in reality, allow yourself to be understood and comforted by your parent. This can have a powerful healing effect.

After doing this for approximately twenty minutes (longer in some cases), you will either feel fatigued or complete for that day. Lie down, take a few deep breaths and let yourself unwind. Sometimes the exercise will feel more powerful than at other times. Every session will be different. Again, if you have a deep history of resentments, the release may take more than a few sessions with each imagined parent, as well as sessions with both your imagined parents together. You should repeat the exercise every few days until you feel your "heavy" resentments lose their intensity and become significantly lighter.

Before you end the exercise, there is one more crucial step. Picture yourself with your parent in a place you would enjoy (such as a park, a beach or perhaps your own home). Imagine a white light sweeping over you and your parent. The light can be seen as emanating from any source comfortable to you —God, universal spirit or your love. Just as warmth and light can assist the healing of a physical wound, so this white light can assist you in healing your emotional relationship with your parent(s). Bask in this light for ten minutes or so as a "treatment."

Do not resume your normal activity until you feel relaxed and complete with the exercise. If you have a lingering pressure in your head or some irritability, take some time to rest and unwind. Be careful not to take your feelings from this exercise out on your loved ones.

3. WRITING THE LETTER
Creative visualization is one way to release old hurts; writing is another. Some people are more visual, others more ver-

bal. I have found it best for people to use both techniques.

Like a diary or private journal, the stream-of-consciousness writing in this exercise is your personal method of uncovering and releasing long-suppressed feelings inside. Use a pen and paper or a typewriter, whichever works better for you. This technique can be especially useful when you are feeling depressed, emotionally or physically shut down, or are in a serious conflict with a boss, lover, spouse or child that may be related to an as yet unresolved dispute with your parents.

Begin your letter with "Dear————," the name you call(ed) your mother or father. Do not worry about neatness, grammar or spelling. While you may find it difficult to express your feelings in words and there may be moments when you feel some resistance holding you back, stick with the exercise and write the most honest, direct and healing letter you can, to each of your parents separately.

If you need to rest after a page or two, go ahead. Feel free to start a letter one day and go back to it later. While you may refer to your list of resentments, this letter should go deeper in expressing your feelings. Wherever there is anger there is hurt. Go underneath your resentments to express your innermost hurts. Don't hold back!

Please note: it is important that you *not* show these letters to your parents. Your purpose is to get the hidden resentments out of your system. Most people find they eventually write ten to thirty pages and are amazed at the deep wells of sadness and pain they have been storing inside.

The following example of a letter from a client named Douglas, a successful advertising executive who had not spoken to his father for more than six years, illustrates the anger and love we keep locked inside.

Dear Dad,

Only now after all these years can I express the pain and loneliness I felt growing up. You and Mom never let us show any emotion. If I was angry you teased me and said I was being a baby. Open anger was impossible or you would punish us for being disrespectful. If I was happy I was told not to be silly. And if, God forbid, I tried to discuss any of my fears or problems with you, I was told to "stop being so weak." It's a wonder Karen and I grew up fairly well-adjusted.

When I was young I remember wondering what you did every day when you went to work. You were always in a rush, always anxious, always quick to anger. I once fantasized that you were some sort of killer, like the bad guys in the Westerns I saw on television. You had us all terrified, especially Mom and Karen. One time when I asked you if you loved us, you said, "Of course I do. I pay the bills, don't I?" For crying out loud, Dad, paying the bills is not love. I wish somehow I could have made you see that I needed something more from a father.

Karen and I were never good enough for you. We both got A's and B's in school, but you were never satisfied. Instead, you said we could do better or that we weren't trying hard enough. You never encouraged us either—you ordered or threatened us. I remember the time I asked for your help on a math problem and you called me stupid. How could you call your own son stupid? Did you think that was going to motivate me?

Even though I never stood up to you in an argument, I could see from the way you criticized and humiliated Mom that you were a bully who would never fight fair. You were always so quick to find fault and you would never listen. No wonder you had to divorce Mom and leave us for that airhead you live with. Now you have no children of your own and you have to live with her spoiled kids.

I think the reason I don't want you in my life is because you would still try to control me. "Be tough, Doug." "Don't let down your guard, Doug." I don't want you to do to my son what you did to me. Adam is a free spirit, a creative little kid with lots of feelings. Probably what you would call a "sissy." He sulks, he giggles, he speaks up when he has something to say, and guess what! He can be sure that no matter what he says or does we will love him. He knows our love is unconditional. Your love wasn't.

Even so, I have to admit I'd get a kick out of seeing you playing with Adam or telling him your stories about when you were a kid. I don't trust you, Dad, but I still have this feeling I've never been able to shake. I almost wish I didn't care about you any more and that I could write you off. But even though it's been a long time, I sometimes miss you. I wonder if I'm not depriving Adam by not letting him see his grandpa.

Your son,
Douglas

Having worked through his resentments, Douglas recognized it was now his choice either to perpetuate the conflict and distance or to let go of his childhood rage and facilitate more caring and understanding. He decided it was time to break the silence and talk to his father face to face. A few days later he called and asked his father to join him for dinner at a restaurant halfway between their two homes. Somewhat hesitant at first, his father agreed to the dinner meeting.

At the restaurant, they were both nervous until Douglas said, "Dad, I'm confident we can have a better relationship now that will be more satisfying for both of us. I'm really glad to see you." With that breaking of the ice, they both relaxed and enjoyed the evening. Soon thereafter, Douglas told me that he had invited his father and his wife for dinner to meet Douglas' wife and Adam, his father's first grandchild.

4. FEELING SUPPORT

A valuable step in self-healing is for you to feel support and encouragement for verbalizing your feelings. Releasing resentments from the past can seem overwhelming at times and can make you feel guilty toward yourself or your parents. It helps to have someone to hear your pain and acknowledge your courage for putting in the effort necessary to make peace with your parents. This next exercise is designed to create support from someone who cares about you.

Select a friend, spouse or sibling whom you trust and who would be willing to sit and listen to you in a very emotional exercise for twenty minutes or longer without interrupting or judging. This friend *should not* be one of your parents. After you are both seated comfortably face to face, your job will be to read your list of resentments or your letter. You might feel embarrassed or reluctant to share these intense feelings. Your friend should be aware that this will not be an easy process for you.

His or her job will be to sit across from you and simply listen. The only words your friend should say are "O.K.," "Tell me more" or "I got it." He or she is not to try to overly comfort you with sympathetic gestures or phrases like "It'll be all right," "Don't cry" or "Cheer up." Rather, it is essential that your listener be there for you without judging, interrupting or glossing over your feelings. Your self-healing occurs from being supported for experiencing your feelings, not from covering over or too quickly dismissing them. The quiet, caring presence of your listener will be the most comforting.

After you have completed your list of resentments and/or your letter, be sure to thank your friend with a hug and possibly an exchange of neck and shoulder massage. His or her support has made it possible for you to work through an important step toward letting go.

5. OVERCOMING YOUR RESISTANCE TO FORGIVENESS

To forgive your parents completely, it is essential that you identify and work through the hidden or unconscious resistances that block your ability to love. This final exercise is a quick and easy way to find out what thoughts and attitudes are working against your intention to make peace with your parents. It will give you the opportunity to draw out the last drops of venom from your emotional abscesses in order to clear these from your system.

Take out a few sheets of paper. On each sheet, draw a vertical line down the center of the page to make two columns. Decide which parent to work on first. Then at the top of one page write "Dear————" (the name you called that parent).

In the left-hand column, you are to write "I FORGIVE YOU." Then close your eyes and notice your immediate thoughts. Do you hear yourself saying something that contradicts the statement "I FORGIVE YOU"? Look for anything sarcastic, doubting or bitter that goes against your intention to forgive. Whatever response comes to mind after "I FORGIVE YOU" should be written in the right-hand column.

In the same fashion, continue to write "I FORGIVE YOU" on the left, as well as your gut responses on the right, until you start to feel a release from the resistance that is holding you back. That resistance is the last remaining obstacle toward completely forgiving your parents and regaining your peace of mind. When you have written three "I FORGIVE YOU's" in a row and can honestly say there are no contradictory or resentful comments in response, then you can take a rest from the exercise. Some people uncover all their resistances in a page of "I FORGIVE YOU" statements. Many find it takes a number of pages or a number of sessions to dissolve all the doubts and conditions that come to mind when we attempt to forgive our parents completely.

The following is a brief example from one person's list of "I FORGIVE YOU" statements and the responses that arose:

Dear Mom:

I forgive you.	No I don't. Not really.
I forgive you.	But I'm still afraid of you.
I forgive you.	Except when you try to manipulate me.
I forgive you.	Only because you make me feel guilty.
I forgive you.	I'd like to, anyway.
I forgive you.	It's not easy after your phone calls.
I forgive you.	But I wish you could see me for who I am and not who you want me to be. If you weren't trying to live through me I could relax more around you.
I forgive you.	Maybe. I don't know.
I forgive you.	This feels strange. Almost numb.
I forgive you.	This is taking too long.
I forgive you.	I wish you'd just know that I love you.
I forgive you.	I care, but it's hard to show you.
I forgive you.	If only I could be sure I was safe to be myself around you.
I forgive you.	[nothing]
I forgive you.	[nothing]
I forgive you.	[nothing]

As an additional completion, you may want to sit down, close your eyes and visualize your parent accepting your forgiveness as he or she says in return: "I'm real sorry that I didn't always love you the way you needed to be loved. It's all right that you were mad at me. I understand. But I was so involved with my own life and my own problems that I didn't have it in me to realize that you were hurting and needed me. I can only ask that you will understand and forgive me."

Breaking Through

Once you begin to forgive your parents and let go of your resentments, a basic shift in your personal growth can ensue. Many patients report that they felt blocked, held back, chronically tense or in a fog prior to working through their resentments. Afterward, you will feel lighter, more complete, whole and centered—in a much better position to clean things up with your real-life parents.

For example, Kathy grew up with parents who rarely respected her right to express her feelings, opinions or independence. When she was a child, her parents bought her a pet beagle that quickly became her closest companion. One day when she returned home from school, however, she was told that her parents had changed their minds—the beagle had been sold and Kathy would never see it again.

"But that was *my* dog," Kathy cried. "You didn't even ask me!"

"What's done is done," her parents responded coldly.

At age twelve, Kathy first began to feel her body changing and was very insecure about her lack of breast development. Sometimes she would lie awake at night worrying and would tell her parents, "I'm flat as a board. Boys will never like me." Her parents' reaction was to send her back to bed with the comment "Don't be ridiculous. You'll be just fine." But Kathy continued to feel awkward and immature next to her busty girlfriends.

That year Kathy's family had a foreign exchange student from Sweden named Lars living at their home. Kathy was very attracted to the handsome thirteen-year-old boy but was too shy to let it show. On one occasion when Kathy and Lars returned from a class picnic soaking wet and shivering from an unexpected rainstorm, Kathy's mother told them both to take off their clothes and wait for her to bring them some warm clothing.

Kathy refused to undress in front of Lars. Even when her mother insisted, "Stop being silly, Katherine. You're going to get sick," she resisted her mother's attempts to remove her soaking-wet blouse. Embarrassed and crying, Kathy had to lock herself in the bathroom in order to change in private.

In another instance, when Kathy was in college her parents disapproved of the young man she was dating. To Kathy's amazement, she later found out that her parents had been using Kathy's best friend as a "spy," obtaining weekly reports on what Kathy did and said with her steady boyfriend. When Kathy discovered her parents' deception, she swore she would never forgive them.

Ten years later when Kathy was in a serious car accident and needed emergency surgery in order to survive, the nurses asked if she wanted someone to contact her parents. Kathy quickly made them promise not to call her mother and father. "I don't want them here," she said. "I don't want to see them."

A few months later, Kathy came to our clinic. She said, "I don't know if I'm capable of having a successful relationship. I feel so blocked emotionally." Her last long-term lover had broken off their three-year relationship just prior to her auto accident. When I asked Kathy why she had not wanted to see her parents in the hospital, she began to cry. "I hate myself for still needing them. Of course I wanted to see them there, but more than that I wanted to be without them. I was afraid they would only blame me and say the accident was my fault because of the people I hang around with."

Kathy discovered as she began to work through her resentments toward her parents that she had been suppressing enormous amounts of anger. She reported after a session visualizing her mother, "I wanted to kill her. A part of me is like an avenging angel that is full of hate and vengeance. I always thought of myself as this 'nice girl,' this 'saint.' Deep inside, there's an ax-murderer that I've not wanted to look at all these years."

After many sessions using the exercises described earlier, Kathy finally gave herself permission to release her angry and violent emotions without feeling guilty. At first she had been reluctant to feel the "ax-murderer" part of herself for fear that she would be hurting her mother. Once I assured her that violent thoughts *do not* mean that you are likely to commit violent actions, Kathy stopped denying the hate and anger she had stuffed inside.

As she commented during one of her sessions, "The only way to really become a 'saint' or just to stop resenting my parents is to make peace with the avenging angel inside. Even though I still can recall times when my parents were very insensitive and even cruel, I don't have to shut down my feelings and become depressed anymore. Letting go of all that pent-up anger has left me feeling more alive and in charge of my life than I've ever felt before."

It's Never Too Late

Edith was fifty-three years old when she consulted me about the severe panic attacks she suffered whenever her eldest daughter asked her to baby-sit for her two-year-old grandchild. From outward appearances, Edith seemed healthy and intelligent, with few complaints about her marriage of thirty-two years. She was proud of her three adult children and could not understand why she felt so anxious.

During her first session, Edith described how "it makes no sense to me whatsoever. All my daughter has to do is ask me to baby-sit and the panic begins. My daughter thinks I'm being selfish and my husband is worried about how upset I get every time we go over there. Part of me thinks I should be a better grandmother, yet if I'm alone with my grand-daughter I can feel my throat and chest tightening and my breathing gets very erratic."

When I took a detailed history, Edith described an incident that had taken place forty-three years earlier, which she had never discussed with anyone. An only child, Edith had been very close to her mother. She recalled, "Mom was always there for me . . . I had her all to myself and she made me feel very special." Then when Edith was ten years old, her mother's sister was killed in a car accident. As soon as Edith's mother brought Edith's three-year-old cousin Yvonne home, life changed radically. Without the customary nine-month pregnancy period to adjust to the prospect of a younger sibling, Edith suddenly had to share her mother, her room and her possessions with her cousin. No longer was she the center of her mother's universe, receiving all her love and affection. Edith resented having to take care of her younger cousin and felt abandoned when her parents adopted Yvonne and gave her special attention.

Thinking about that childhood incident, Edith commented, "But that was so long ago. How could it be causing my current panic?"

I explained that whenever Edith was asked to baby-sit or

be alone with her granddaughter, it triggered the buried emotions she had never been allowed to express about Yvonne coming to stay. "In those moments you may be feeling the same suppressed rage you held inside when you were ten years old. You had no means of expressing your upset over having your 'childhood paradise' with your mother taken away. After all, 'poor Yvonne' needed your mother's love more than you did."

Edith recalled having had similar feelings of anxiety and agitation when she was alone with her children while they were very young. "But then I just told myself not to let anything get in the way of taking care of them. When raising my own children, I simply had to keep my feelings inside." Since she had less of an obligation to baby-sit for her grand-child, her defenses were weaker and the long-suppressed feelings could now surface.

At first Edith was reluctant to let herself get too involved in the exercises to work through her resentments, claiming, "I'm too old for this and my mother's been dead for fifteen years." When she made a list of resentments, however, she described a "torrent of angry feelings I never imagined were inside me." Beating a pillow and shouting how she felt "left out," "cheated" and "taken for granted," Edith began to visualize her mother acknowledging her feelings of hurt and abandonment for the first time.

Releasing her resentments and forgiving her mother, Edith reached a new level of understanding about her own emotional make-up. She discovered that she had built an emotional wall to protect herself and realized "it's no wonder my daughters have accused me of being cold and unfeeling. Even though I resented my mother's lack of affection, I've become the same type of person."

As part of her making peace, I asked Edith to research her mother's family background to see if she could better understand her mother's psychology. During a long conversation with a distant cousin Edith hadn't spoken to for years, she discovered that a family pattern of abandonment and feelings of rejection had been passed down from generation to generation. Edith learned that her grandmother had died when Edith's mother was a young girl. When her grandfather remarried, Edith's mother was forced to endure a brutal disciplinarian stepmother who resented the attention Edith's mother was given by her own father. Finally, Edith's mother was taken in by her great-aunt. Just as Edith's mother had been "rescued" by a warm-hearted relative, so was she determined to "rescue" Yvonne. In fact, as Edith's mother was dying, one of the last things she said was "I've tried so hard to be good to children that need me. It's the most important thing I've done."

Understanding the family legacy helped Edith recognize that forces beyond her mother's control had influenced her apparent rejection of Edith. Whereas Edith had always suppressed her resentments toward her mother and Yvonne, she could now appreciate the unfortunate hurt she had suffered. Instead of letting her long-suppressed rage continue to cause panic attacks and a fear of "what might happen" with her grandchild, Edith realized the time had come to break through the family pattern.

Working with Edith and her eldest daughter, I began to help them tear down the emotional barriers that had kept them separate. Edith's daughter described how "seeing Mom start to open up has been terrific for our relationship. None of us ever understood why she was so reluctant to show her feelings or why she got so anxious about baby-sitting."

As a result of understanding and working through the suppressed incident from her childhood, Edith was gradually able to eliminate her fear of being alone with her grandchild. In most cases, strong phobias or anxiety reactions take time to heal. Expressing resentments is not a "magical" cure; Edith still had to learn to deal with her fears and anxieties whenever they reappeared.

At first she began to baby-sit only when her husband was present. Then she agreed to one hour alone with her grandchild. Soon it was two hours. Gradually Edith broke through her fear and was able to baby-sit without feeling anxious or afraid. More important, with tears in her eyes she described her joy at being able to spend more time with her children and grandchildren. "I had thought that making a list of resentments was nothing more than dredging up the past. Now I see that by facing up to the incidents in my childhood, I've learned how to be a more affectionate and loving person . . . and that it's never too late to get closer to the people I love."

3

Expressing Anger and Love with Your Family

Many of us grew up in families in which it was not all right for children to get angry. If you were upset and raised your voice to your parents, the reaction was

> "How dare you talk to your mother [or father] that way."
> "You don't appreciate all that I've done for you."
> "Show some respect."
> "You don't love me."

The either/or thinking in most families is that you *either* love your parents *or* you are angry with them. Anger and love, however, inevitably go together. One of the greatest insights of Sigmund Freud, which will stand the test of time, is that all human emotional relationships, especially our most intimate, are ambivalent—*where there is intense love there is also the opportunity for intense anger.* Shutting down your anger and keeping the lid on your emotions blocks not only your anger but also your ability to love.

For instance, Nancy is a client of mine who grew up in a volatile Irish Catholic family in which her father frequently got his way by intimidating others with his fiery temper and booming voice. Nancy recalled that when his face turned beet red, her mother and older brothers would cringe in fear. At any moment her father was going to explode. More than anything, Nancy dreaded the insulting remarks her father made when he was angry, and she did everything she could to avoid incurring his wrath.

She also decided that anger was something she should never express. Not only was Nancy, like most women, raised to believe that a "nice girl" does not get angry, but she feared that her rage, if expressed, could hurt someone as she and her family had been hurt. Throughout her unhappy first marriage and in a series of frustrating jobs in which she felt mistreated and underpaid, Nancy did her best to keep her mouth shut and her feelings stiffly in check.

Yet by the time Nancy was thirty years old, she found herself chronically depressed and lonely and did not know why. The protective wall she had built around her emotions meant that her relationships, especially those with men and with her parents, were "arm's-length" and emotionally distant.

After she made a list of resentments and worked through most of them on her own, Nancy expected that the problems with her family would be resolved. During her next visit with her parents, however, Nancy discovered that even though she had begun to change herself by releasing her resentments, her parents were still the same. Her father still intimidated her with his anger. Her mother continued to discourage any outward display of affection. As much as Nancy wanted things to be different with her family, she found herself unable to change the anxious and self-contained way she related to her mother and father.

As Nancy described it, "I love my parents, but I don't know how to be myself when I'm with them. Every time I'm there I either get a headache or stomach ache trying to avoid doing or saying anything that will upset them."

Like Nancy, many people feel in a rut with their parents. You want to love them, but something always gets in the way. You want to learn to accept them more, yet nagging traits still grate on your nerves. You want to be friends with them, but you find instead that the old roles and conflicts from childhood reappear. In spite of your intention to "get along this time," you are soon embroiled in yet another dispute or anxious confrontation.

To see how this applies in your family, ask yourself *honestly* to what extent you enjoy your family get-togethers:

—Are the visits relaxed and loving, or do you dread some aspect of being with your parents?

—Are the special occasions (birthdays, holidays, etc.) a time for celebration or a mere obligation?

—Do you feel you are at your best with your parents, or do you get stuck in a childhood or adolescent role you thought you had outgrown years ago (such as being defensive, wanting approval, shutting down, feeling helpless)?

—Do you frequently experience family conflict and communication problems?

For many people, the perpetual battles and discomforts they have with their parents seem almost inevitable. Even the most ambitious and creative people have been known to say about their relationship with their parents, "I'm just trying to make the best of an unfortunate situation."

This chapter will give you the tools to change that gloomy outlook. Rather than being a victim with your mother and father, you will discover your opportunity for control and power. Rather than being forced to endure a less than tolerable situation at your meetings with your parents, you can establish the degrees of honesty, acceptance and enjoyment you deserve. Rather than stuffing away your anger, as well as your love, you can learn in this chapter how to make anger healthy and how to share more love with your family.

A Change in Perspective

Prior to working through your resentments using the exercises in Chapter Two, visits with your parents were undoubtedly restricted by the amount of effort it took to keep your resentments inside. However, working through your resentments is only the first step. Even though you may have healed some of the emotional hurts from your childhood, your parents are still the same. Without a change in perspective, your visits with them might still consist of

—Hoping they won't do or say the things that will revive old hurts and resentments.

—Feeling out of control when they want you to play the same roles you played for them as a child.

—Blaming and resenting them for the traits, behavior and attitudes they have had for a lifetime.

—Wanting desperately to escape from their influence, rules and habits so that you can be your own person.

—Expecting and wishing they would change.

Just because you have begun to make peace with your inner parents, that does not mean that your relationship with your actual parents is going to change overnight. Until you acquire the skills for expressing anger constructively and getting your needs from them better met, you will fall back into the same old patterns. You will need to be both tender *and* firm, loving *and* strong, to put your increased awareness and good intentions into practice.

The change in perspective is essentially the process of transforming an adult-child or powerful-powerless relationship into an adult-adult relationship of equals. If you have a child's perspective or feel powerless when dealing with your parents, you may find yourself trying to avoid making a scene, fearing confrontations and avoiding any emotional issues, or thinking that it is not worth the trouble because your parents will sooner or later be gone. Even if you are a parent yourself, you may still be relating to your own parents with the helpless, burdened or "I'm not responsible for what goes on" attitude of a child. By blaming them for what you don't enjoy in the relationship and by remaining passive in letting the problems persist, you give up your right to improve things with your parents. Even though you may accuse your parents of "forcing you" to submit to their wishes, the actuality is that you *choose* to give up your power by the way you view the relationship.

I often remind patients that *complaining is an ineffective way of getting what you want in life.* If your primary response to your parents is to feel victimized, trapped or resentful, it is no wonder there have been no improvements in the relationship. By assuming that *they* have control of your happiness and satisfaction, you have guaranteed that you will continue to be stuck in a miserable rut.

On the other hand, if you are willing to *take 100 percent of the responsibility for what transpires between you,* enormously different results will occur. Now that you are an adult, your needs, good ideas and empathy become the keys to making your relationship with your mother and father more honest, fun, relaxed and healthy. Rather than being stuck in past resentments and behavior patterns, you can take the initiative to begin building a relationship that is more satisfying for *both* you and your parents.

Breaking Free of the Approval Trap

Stop for a moment and ask yourself why you and your parents have conflicts in the first place. Is there something inherently stressful about the relationship between parents and their adult children? The answer, all too frequently, is yes.

In your relationship with your parents, it is as though there are four separate characters in every two-person interaction. For instance, between you and your father there are

1. Your father's expectations of who you "should" be.
2. You, yourself.
3. Your expectations of who your father "should" be.
4. Your father, himself.

At any given moment, you may be in conflict with your father because

—You're not living up to his expectations.
—He isn't living up to your expectations.

—You're tired of having to live up to his expectations.
—He's tired of having to live up to your expectations.

Even though you and your father would both like to have a relationship based on unconditional love, the fact remains that *your feelings for him are quite often conditional* (as to how he conforms to your expectations and needs) and *his feelings for you are conditional* (based on how you conform to his expectations and needs).

This "approval trap," which is the major cause of nearly every dispute and stressful situation with your parents, can limit your enjoyment and block your feelings of love because it restricts you to the following:

—Wishing they were different.
—Resenting that they are not.
—Resisting their advice and attempts to help you.
—Feeling trapped by their expectations.
—Feeling driven to defy or conform to their values.
—Feeling defensive and unloving when you are with them.

In order to break free of the approval trap, you must first stop resisting the fact that both you and your parents have conditions and expectations. An important fact of life is that *all growth involves the integration of seemingly opposite values* —the only way to have unconditional love is to recognize and admit you sometimes have conditions blocking your love. We must learn to be more accepting of our own and other people's conditions. Becoming aware of this paradox allows you to stop being controlled by your value judgments of your parents and their value judgments of you.

Changing "Have To's" into "Want To's"

If you take your parents' expectations and conditions too seriously, your daily life will be filled with attempts to resist or give in to their values. Such either/or thinking implies "Either do what they say or you will lose their love and respect." It is not surprising to find that people in their forties, fifties and sixties continue to work themselves to death, to resent their bosses and to feel unfulfilled because they are subconsciously still trying to please their parents. On the other hand, there are many individuals who spend their entire lives trying desperately to get back at their parents by defying them. Whether you are a conformer or a rebel, to live your life in reaction to your parents' expectations or "have to's" is a form of imprisonment that will keep you dissatisfied and unfulfilled.

Your parents are but two of several advisers and supporters in your life. Sometimes their suggestions are excellent; at other times they are simply inappropriate to your need or situation. When you realize that deep down you will continue loving your parents no matter what and that deep down they will continue loving you no matter what, the "have to" disappears. You can choose to accept their advice or not. In order to change your day-to-day relationship with your parents from a series of "have to's" into self-initiated "want to's," you need to realize that while your parents may resist, protest and disapprove of your independent decisions, their advice need not govern you. If you remain calm and centered, you will see despite differences your love can continue.

Setting Limits

Carol's problem with her parents is a good illustration. Even though Carol, thirty-six and divorced, was successful in her career as a graphic designer and self-supporting in her handsomely decorated apartment, her mother would call nearly every day, according to Carol, "Just to see if I'm all right." Each phone call would at some point revert to the same issue that drove Carol up the wall, as her mother would say somberly, "Your father misses you and wishes you'd come to visit more often. You don't want to hurt him, do you?"

Before she worked out her resentments, Carol had perceived each of her mother's requests as a guilt-ridden imposition, a "have to" that implied "Do what I say or else you'll hurt your parents." With each "have to," Carol would become more resentful as she felt, "I've asked my mother a thousand times not to call me every day. She interrupts me when I'm eating breakfast or dinner . . . sometimes when I'm in bed with a man. And that guilt trip about hurting my father . . . if he wants me to visit, why doesn't he pick up the phone and call?"

Carol was clearly feeling victimized by her relationship with her parents, as though she were nothing more than a helpless child. I pointed out to Carol that she did not have to remain a resentful and powerless child at the mercy of her parents' needs and wishes. Carol had an opportunity to be more effective in the relationship: to apply tools and principles that would allow the relationship to become more of what *she* wanted it to be; to be more accountable for the results and to be more creative in offering solutions.

For years Carol had felt self-righteous in her victim role, as if saying, "See what they do to me!" Now she had to face up to the fact that phone calls with her mother left her feeling angry, guilt-ridden and sometimes depressed. When I asked Carol what she would prefer, she knew she wanted more independence *and* better communication with her parents. Yet she was afraid that if she "rocked the boat" and expressed her anger she would sacrifice her parents' approval and love. She was allowing the approval trap to block her relationship with her parents.

Carol had always resented her parents for not being more sensitive to *her* needs, yet she had never seen the opportunity of being more sensitive to *their* needs, in seeing more deeply what motivated their behavior. Like most people, she believed that the only "nice" way to deal with her parents was to ignore them or avoid a confrontation. At the same time, she could see how putting up emotional defenses against her parents was making her relationship with them even worse.

I told Carol that using anger constructively means putting an end to the things that irritate her, while at the same time being sensitive to her parents' needs. When I asked her why her mother called so often, Carol knew immediately: "She misses me. She's suffering from the empty-nest syndrome with all four kids grown and living on their own. She's worried about me, because she thinks I'm as helpless and afraid to be on my own as she was before she met my father."

Then I suggested to Carol that she offer her mother a solution in which both Carol *and* her mother could get more of what they needed and wanted. "Instead of stifling your anger at the way your mother expresses her concern for you, use the anger as a call to action—*to propose a solution that will be effective.*" It was the first time Carol began to see anger as something other than a destructive emotion that had to be suppressed.

A few days later Carol's mother phoned her at the office and interrupted her in the middle of an important meeting. When Carol returned the call, she decided not to hide her irritation and said, "Mom, it makes me angry when you call me at the office. You know I love you a lot and I understand that your calling me every day is a sign of how much you care. *And* since I need my independence, I want you to do something for me. What would work much better is if I called you or you called me once or maybe twice a week. Then we can keep each other up to date and have some good, comfortable talks. Let's try for the next few weeks to make our conversations really enjoyable, all right?"

At first Carol's mother resisted. She stopped calling at the office but increased her calls to Carol's apartment. Once again Carol decided to be firm. "Mom, I'm angry with the number of times you call. I love you and I want to be close to you. *And* if we talk on the phone once or twice a week, I think we'll be closer, with fewer disagreements, than if we talk every day. We'll both enjoy our communications more." Even though Carol's mother didn't approve of Carol's being angry at her, she eventually agreed to the plan and followed it with only rare exceptions from then on.

Note that Carol said *"and"* instead of "but" when describing what she needed from her mother. When you say to your parents "I love you, *but,*" it is a coercive statement, which implies "I won't love you *unless* you do what I say." On the other hand, when you say "I love you *and* I'd like you to do such and such," it communicates that you will love your parents *no matter what* (unconditional love) *and* that you sincerely need them to do something for you, according to your preferences. The "I love you, but" is really a complaint and tends to elicit resentment and resistance because none of us likes to have love used against us as a form of emotional blackmail. "I love you *and*" communicates both unconditional love and what you specifically need, which tends to get much better results.

It is not just what you say but how you say it. You *can* set limits with your parents when you are coming from an attitude of love and sensitivity to their needs. When you are defensive, critical or judgmental, no amount of discussion will result in a solution both you and your parents can enjoy.

In Carol's case, her breakthrough with her mother carried over into her relationships with men. Prior to working through her resentments and learning to use anger constructively, Carol was involved in nothing but "arm's-length" relationships in which she would date more than one man at a time, never get too emotionally involved and act defensively and defiantly. After she was able to feel more love for her parents and calmly but firmly set limits with them, she began to see her power in relationships differently. Rather than being cold and defensive in order to protect her independence, Carol began to let down her defenses and became more able to ask for and get what she wanted.

Carol had also been afraid that "if I let people know I love them, they will use it against me." This was especially the case with her ex-husband, Thomas, whom Carol had avoided seeing for more than two years. Recently Carol invited Thomas out for dinner "just to stay in contact and reestablish our friendship." After an elegant meal at a fine restaurant, Carol went home feeling triumphant. As she told me later, "I saw that I loved him *and* that I didn't want to be married to him anymore. I felt strong and in charge this time. I even told him that I had missed him, knowing that there was no danger in showing him some affection."

Beyond the Blame Game

Before Carol discovered how to ask for what she wanted and express her anger constructively, her reaction to her parents had always been to shut down her feelings and blame her mother and father for her discomfort. Rather than working through their differences, she and her parents would resort to psychological weapons to manipulate each other. Carol became an expert at sulking, blaming, withdrawing her love or acting like a martyr. Yet her parents were just as good, if not better, at suffering like martyrs, trying to make Carol feel guilty and never getting what they wanted either. *In a family relationship that isn't working,* everyone *feels like "poor me."*

When you and your parents are each trying to change the other's behavior by complaining, blaming and feeling victimized, it is a no-win situation. The most that can happen is that both sides relieve some of their own guilt and frustration. Remember, what you resist persists. The more you try to put your parents in the wrong, the more they will have to prove to you that they are right! The more you resist them as they are, the more their traits will annoy you.

The paradox is that if you want the relationship to change and improve, you need to accept your parents exactly as they are. Acceptance and understanding make a better basis for change than annoyance and blame. Carol could not change her mother's need to call her or her mother's "empty-nest syndrome" through rejection and blame. Yet, through being loving and strong, she could create a solution that fulfilled her own need for more independence and her mother's need for contact and appreciation. Rather than blaming her mother for the problem, Carol was able to use her anger constructively and commit her energy to a positive outcome.

Receptive Listening

Quite often I hear people complain that their parents "never listen" or "refuse to understand me." Yet we often fail to realize that our parents have just as great a need for *us* to listen to and understand *them.* "As ye sow, so shall ye reap." You must learn to generate a more receptive, less reactive atmosphere. Until you begin to stop judging, criticizing and shutting off your parents, how can you expect them to be more attentive to you?

Receptive listening can assist you to improve your relationship with your parents dramatically. Most of us learned poor communications skills when we were young, especially when it came to understanding and expressing feelings. We often send messages that are vague, ambiguous, contradictory and difficult to follow. By paying attention to your own listening habits, you can discover a number of ways to break through the communication barriers you have with your parents.

The art of receptive listening is one of the powerful ways we communicate our love. There are three components to receptive listening: developing empathy, overcoming self-righteousness and staying relaxed.

DEVELOPING EMPATHY
Empathy is defined in *Webster's New Collegiate Dictionary* as "the capacity for participation in another's feelings or ideas." It means listening to your parents in such a way that you can

understand the feelings underneath the words and can share their frame of reference. Just as you would not want to criticize your parents for saying "I don't like cauliflower," so it is pointless to resent or try to change them when they express a feeling or opinion such as "I don't think couples should live together if they're not married," "I don't understand why you let your teenagers wear their hair like that" or "I don't think you should dress like that. What will people think?"

Rather than blaming or attacking them for their opinions, you can look at the feelings, experiences and attitudes that underlie their words. Instead of shouting "How can you say that? That's so old-fashioned," you might discover that if you had shared the same background, values and upbringing as your parents, you would perhaps hold the same opinion. A good indicator that you are listening empathically is when you are able to say to your parents "I understand" or "I can see how you feel that way."

However, that does not mean you have to agree with everything your parents assert about the way you should conduct your life. It simply gives them the safety and acceptance that we all need when expressing our feelings. If your parents know that you can understand and appreciate their point of view, they will be far less likely to try to impose it on you. Remember again the principle of "what you resist persists" ; the less you oppose and deny your parents' feelings and experiences, the less your differences will require arguments and conflicts.

Whenever you feel yourself becoming impatient, judgmental or critical of your parents' feelings and opinions, consider for a moment how you would feel if you "walked a mile in their shoes." Instead of resisting their ideas, you can learn a lot about them and yourself by asking questions that will help you understand how and why they feel that way.

Many clients have expressed the fear that "if I let them have their say, they'll think I'm in complete agreement." This need not be the case. If you listen empathically and take the time to understand your parents' feelings fully, you will create an opportunity to explain calmly why you hold a different point of view. Only if you have given your parents the love, support and appreciation of hearing them out can they begin to understand and appreciate your frame of reference.

OVERCOMING SELF-RIGHTEOUSNESS

Most arguments between people and their parents have little, if anything, to do with the words being used or the ideas being discussed. For instance, you and your parents may be having a debate about politics, women's rights, the latest fashion in clothes or the significance of a recent film. Yet the anger and heated words are less about the issue and more about the fundamental question of "who's right?"

In many families the underlying conflict in every argument is a bitter competition over who has the power, who has the authority. It is usually a fight for control, with both sides feeling misunderstood.

We human beings are very self-righteous. It seems to be a part of our nature that we want to be right and have things our way. Especially in a heated argument, we are sure that we're right and the other person is wrong. We create for ourselves a Greek chorus of friends and allies to reflect back to us how right and wonderful we are and how wrong and awful the other person is.

Rather than using each discussion with your parents as a vehicle for proving how right you can be, receptive listening allows you to give your parents the opportunity to be right as well. If you insist "I'm right and you're wrong," they will feel required to fight back and say "*I'm* right and *you're* wrong." On the other hand, empathic listening allows for the cultivation of "point of view" —appreciating how each of us is right from our own perspective. Especially when it comes to feelings, no one is wrong. An important aspect of intimacy is to value and accept seemingly opposing points of view.

When you are acting self-righteous with your parents, your communication style consists of

—Showing your impatience with everything they say.
—Interrupting at every opportunity.
—Never giving in even if what they say makes sense.
—Making them feel guilty, stupid or old-fashioned.
—Fighting for your position as if your life depends on it.

When you are listening receptively, your intention is for your parents to feel more relaxed, appreciated and understood. Your communication style consists of

—Reflecting warmth in your body posture, eye contact, voice tone and facial expressions.
—Asking thoughtful questions to better understand their point of view.
—Appreciating the feelings that underlie their words.
—Calmly reflecting back to them their feelings without adding on, judging or criticizing. If you can repeat their point of view using phrases like "I can see how . . . ," "I understand that you feel . . ." or "I appreciate your

saying . . . ," your parent will be more likely to see your point of view as well.

Remember that the issue between you and your parents is not who wins and who loses but rather to make peace, to create a win-win situation. If you see yourself reacting without listening, you must be the one to take the initiative to stop, slow down, relax and ask your parents to restate or rephrase their point of view. Even if some of the things they say still get on your nerves, it is your responsibility to let them know you are making a sincere effort to listen to and appreciate their point of view. Only when you stop resisting your parents is there any chance that they will stop persisting in whatever upsets you. If you resist your parents' opinion or point of view, they will be more likely to persist in proving to you how right they are. Once you have shown your parents that they are being heard and understood, the conflict can more easily be resolved.

STAYING RELAXED

Many people report that they generally feel tense and defensive with their parents. They simply accept that when they are with their mother or father, it is "normal" to feel that way.

In order to listen receptively and avoid unnecessary conflicts with your parents, it is essential that you employ whatever relaxation techniques work best for you to reduce your stress level and let down your own defenses. If you approach your get-togethers, phone calls and discussions with anxiety, you are more likely to find yourself reacting defensively to each potentially upsetting thing your parents might say.

By discovering how to relax, you will be far more successful in communicating effectively and listening receptively. If you notice that your chest is constricted, your shoulders held tightly and your breathing short, find an opportunity to stretch, go for a walk or jog.

Regular periods of relaxation lead one to become less reactive and volatile. The daily practice of meditation, especially the TM (Transcendental Meditation) technique, exposes the mind and body to a unique state of deep rest that appears to have a profound healing effect upon the psyche. Just as bed rest helps the body to repair physical wounds, the inner rest achieved through TM appears to facilitate the healing of psychological wounds.

If you set aside twenty minutes to do TM or another form of relaxation just prior to your visits and phone calls with your parents, you will discover that you can enjoy and appreciate your discussions far more than if you approach them with a chip on your shoulder or a sense of foreboding anxiety. By relaxing and reducing your stress levels prior to and during your get-togethers, you will be far less likely to turn a minor incident into another frustrating dispute.

Expressing Your Anger Effectively

Sometimes being relaxed, avoiding blame and having an open mind still fall short when your parents step on your toes (metaphorically) in a way that makes you exclaim "Ouch!" Even when this happens, maintaining a positive outlook, setting limits, listening receptively and having empathy can assist you to express your anger constructively and effectively.

When you were younger, it probably was not safe to get angry when your parents hurt your feelings. You either got hit, grounded, sent to your room or in other ways punished for "talking back." Over the years you may have learned to hold in your anger, to keep hurt feelings stuffed inside and to find indirect ways to strike back at those who hurt you.

In the process of making peace with your parents, you have to expect that they may surprise you or simply upset you with statements or behavior that make you angry. No one likes to be judged or reproached, especially by someone he or she loves. If anger toward your parents could be expressed quickly and effectively, it wouldn't be too much of a problem. In most cases, however, we are immobilized or terrified by the anger we feel for someone as close as our mother or father.

The reasons we suppress and contain our anger are many. Most of us simply fear losing control. Some are afraid they will look foolish if they show they are upset. Others are afraid they will hurt or offend someone they love. Still others feel guilty and uncomfortable simply having angry thoughts.

When your parents upset you, you have two choices—you can turn your upset into hostile anger or into effective anger. Hostile anger comes in a variety of forms. Some people suppress their feelings, smile when they are angry and hold on to resentments until one day they explode in a hurtful and inappropriate outburst of feelings. Some people become physically ill from the anger inside them. Others secretly dwell on their hurt feelings and carry on hostile conversations in their minds. Still others express hostile anger with a bitter assault of harsh words to punish anyone who has offended or hurt them. Many simply take out their negative feelings on loved ones, employees or strangers. Whether you scream in rage or walk out in cold silence, the goal of hostile anger is always the same—sooner or later to punish your parents, directly or indirectly, for being insensitive to your feelings.

The results of hostile anger are almost always negative. By attacking your parents, you force them to be more defensive. By masking your real feelings of love and hurt with self-righteousness or cold indifference, you escalate the conflict. By creating emotional distance, you increase the communication problems.

On the other hand, anger becomes effective when you handle it less reactively. Instead of blaming or insulting, your goal is to take responsibility for your own hurt feelings, describe your upset and have your parent understand you. Without attacking the other person or holding your feelings inside, you can stand up for yourself by quickly saying, in essence, "That hurt, here's why and here's what I need so I won't be hurt again." Expressing anger effectively increases the trust and love in your relationship because you are willing to admit "I care about you and it hurts me when . . ."

Effective anger is warm. You show by your eye contact, choice of words and tone of voice that despite being angry, you still care about your parents' feelings. State your concern by explaining, in your own words, "This is important, and because I love you and you love me, we need to clean it up." Avoid personal attacks, accusations or statements that say "You did this" or "You are that." Never say "never" or "always."

Effective anger is specific. Avoid lecturing, intimidating or trying to change your parent when expressing your anger. There is no value in dwelling on the past or bringing up unrelated incidents to buttress your "case." The sooner you can express exactly why you feel hurt, the sooner you can begin to release the feelings of anger. Start by saying "I care about our relationship and I feel hurt when _____ happens." Let him or her know exactly the specific change you want to see.

Effective anger is receptive. Once you have had a chance to explain why you felt hurt, let your parents talk. Without interrupting, try to understand how they feel. Allow them to release their anger and feel understood. If their point of view is still unclear to you, ask for clarification. Your ability to see their vantage point as well as your own can produce constructive change.

The following case will illustrate how to effectively express anger with your family.

When Mark was growing up as the middle son in a fiercely competitive household near Philadelphia, he was considered the "black sheep" in the family. While his older brother became a doctor and his younger brother studied to be a lawyer, Mark set off on a different course. After college he joined the Peace Corps, later worked as a special education teacher and eventually became the director of an innovative school for children with learning disabilities.

In spite of Mark's unique and hard-earned success, his parents never stopped pressuring him to conform to their standards. Mark describes his visits home: "They go on and on about my brother the doctor and the new house he bought for his wife and two kids. Or they recite glorious tales of my brother the lawyer and all the big-name clients he's defended. When they get around to me, it's always 'When are you getting married?' 'Did you call your aunt when she was in the hospital?' 'Are you making any money at that school of yours?' and 'You're almost forty . . . when are you going to get serious about your future?' "

For the past three years Mark has been living with Laura,

an artist who grew up in Texas and has two children from a previous marriage. According to Mark, "When I brought Laura and her children to meet my family it was a total disaster. Mom was determined not to like Laura and made little effort to hide her judgments. She made sarcastic comments about Laura's clothes, her Southern accent and the 'permissive' way she raises her children. My brothers were no different as they talked down to Laura, excluded her from conversations and asked me privately, 'Why do you want to spend your time with someone else's kids?' I wanted to tell them all just where to go, but I decided to keep my mouth shut and pray the visit would soon be over."

When Mark's mother called to invite him to spend Christmas with the family again this year, she failed to mention Laura or the children. Mark asked his mother, "What about Laura?" His mother snapped, "What *about* Laura? Can't you come without her?" As soon as Mark related the conversation to Laura, she became furious. "It hurts that your mother doesn't like me. If you have to go, then you may as well go without me and the kids." Mark felt caught in a bind. He couldn't say no to his family, yet he wanted to spend Christmas with Laura and the children. Asking Laura to give his family another chance and join him on the trip, Mark was surprised to hear Laura tell him, "As long as you let your mother get away with her rudeness, I'd rather not see her." In conflict and depressed, Mark came to see me.

In our sessions together, Mark began by working through a host of resentments toward his parents and brothers that he had never previously expressed. The cold reception for Laura was only one of dozens of incidents in which Mark felt hurt or belittled by his family. Even though Mark was able to release many resentments, his anger and frustration over the current dilemma left him feeling immobilized. "I'm damned if I do and damned if I don't" was his attitude.

When I asked Mark if he had ever gotten angry with his mother, he thought for a moment and said, "We've had our arguments, but I've never really told her when I've been upset." In this case, however, holding his anger inside was no longer a viable choice. Mark said that his stomach felt like it was tied in knots and that he had become increasingly short-tempered with Laura and the children. The time had come for him to learn how to stand up for himself with his family.

As part of his treatment, I encouraged Mark to express his anger to me in a role-playing exercise as though I were his mother. At first Mark held back, saying, "I can't raise my voice to my mother." I asked him to imagine what might happen if he did release his anger toward his family. Mark said he was afraid of hurting his mother, yet he admitted that expressing his anger in an exercise couldn't hurt her. Recognizing that he didn't need to act out his rage toward her in person, he then let himself get involved in the role-playing exercise. Shaking his fists, swearing and shouting, Mark hurled a tirade of feelings at me as I played his mother. He shouted such things as:

"You don't care about anyone but yourself."
"Quit telling me how to run my life!"
"I hate it when you judge and criticize every person I bring home to meet you."
"I have a right to be different!"
"Don't lay your fears and insecurities on me!"

Once he had let off steam and felt good about having released his anger, I suggested that we switch roles with Mark playing his mother and me playing Mark. Then I initiated the following conversation to help Mark see the problem from his mother's point of view.

Mark (played by me): Could you please explain to me why you've been so cold and critical to Laura and her children?

Mother (played by Mark): You really want to know? I'll tell you. First of all, I don't like the fact that she's already been married. Why doesn't the childrens' father pay their share instead of depending on you?

Then there's the way she looks. Very sexy and alluring. Not the kind of proper woman I had in mind for you.

Mark (played by me): Are you jealous?

Mother (played by Mark): That's not why I don't like her. She's not very educated and she's got that Texas drawl. I'm embarrassed to be seen with her. And you tell me she's an artist but she's not making a living at it. You don't have that much money to waste, do you?

Mark (played by me): Mom, you have so many judgments and criticisms of Laura. Why is she so important to you?

Mother (played by Mark): Important? She's living with my son. And I want to make sure she's not going to take advantage of you or hurt you.

Mark (played by me):   Why do you care?

Mother (played by Mark):   Because I love you.

Mark (played by me):   You do?

Mother (played by Mark):   Of course I do. Otherwise I wouldn't care who you were with. I love you very much and want you to be happy.

At this point we stopped the role-playing exercise because Mark had discovered that underneath the disapproval is our parents' love and concern for our happiness. As I described it to Mark, "Your mother's pressuring and unsolicited opinions are her way of loving you. She is simply expressing her values and vantage point about what she thinks will make you happy. Another person's opinions or values don't have to control you. You can let your mother have her point of view without trying to change her. Otherwise, the more you resist her point of view and try to convince her she's wrong, the more she will persist in trying to convince you she's right!"

Having a Peace Talk

A few weeks before Christmas, Mark flew to Philadelphia for a convention and arranged to meet his mother so they could spend some time together. He told her that he wanted to discuss the Christmas holidays and began by saying, "I love you, Mom, and it means a lot to me to spend Christmas with you and Dad and the family. My family now includes Laura and her two children. While I know you might not approve of Laura or the fact that we're living together, I want you to know that it hurts me to see her rejected by the family. Laura and I love each other . . . I'd feel much better about Christmas if we could all spend it together."

Having expressed his feelings without blame or criticism, Mark listened without interrupting while his mother described *her* anger at him for living with Laura. As she spoke, Mark made a conscious effort to remain relaxed, attentive and receptive. Watching his mother closely, he was able to see the concern and love underneath her angry words and criticisms. When his mother was done talking, Mark gave her a hug and said, "Mom, you're very special to me. You're entitled to your feelings and opinions as I am to mine. Laura wants you to like her and I hope someday you will. You've done your job as parent by sharing with me your concerns and now you can relax. I am responsible for and feel good about my decisions. Even though I don't always do things the way you and Dad would like, I want you both to know I love you."

When he discussed the visit with Laura, she began to see that Mark valued his relationship with her and the children enough to stand up to his mother's disapproval. Because Mark was able to listen to Laura's feelings of discomfort and anger toward his mother without feeling attacked or becoming defensive, the problem with his family was no longer a problem in his relationship with Laura. Both Mark and Laura knew that in the process of making peace with his parents, Mark was doing the best he could. Feeling that their commitment to each other was solid, they became less affected by what Mark's mother thought about their relationship.

Even with some difficult moments, the visit with Mark's family was enjoyable. When Mark's mother made a comment about Laura's clothes, neither Laura nor Mark had as big an emotional reaction as they had had the previous year. Both realized that change comes slowly and does not happen all at once. For Mark, the highlight of the Christmas get-together came at the airport when his mother gave Laura a farewell hug and said, "Take good care of my son for me. He loves you and the children a great deal."

In Mark's conflict with his family and in hundreds of other cases, anger tends to accumulate with each phone call and visit. Even though Mark got the result he wanted—his mother and Laura became more friendly toward each other —he nevertheless continued to experience irritation at a number of his mother's statements and actions. The process of making peace with our parents reminds me of the Buddhist quote about enlightenment: "Before enlightenment, you carry water and chop wood. After enlightenment, you carry water and chop wood."

Even though Mark had made tremendous progress in healing his resentments toward his parents, he still had to learn other techniques for effectively discharging his rage. Part of making peace with your parents is recognizing that further conflict and communication problems will arise. Dealing with them constructively is the key.

Discharging Rage Appropriately

When your parent says or does something that makes you want to scream and you don't do anything, your body suffers from the contradiction. Half your muscles tense as if to strike back in anger while the other half work doubly hard to suppress your reaction. It's like trying to drive with your foot on the brake.

In addition to the physical stress of holding in anger, you pay the price of reduced sensitivity to your most tender feelings. The usual way we disguise anger for our parents is with indifference ("Angry? I'm not angry!"). The energy you put into holding back your feelings toward your parents can easily hold back your spontaneity, warmth and ability to enjoy your loved ones as well. Simply rationalizing your upsets or trying to shrug them off will only build up more tension. Letting go of your feelings of rage safely and privately is an essential skill for learning to communicate with your parents.

Every once in a while Mark's mother would call him with some request or comment that made him angry. After one such call, I suggested he close the door to his bedroom, visualize his mother's face and shout "Get off my back!" while jumping up and down. When I first suggested this simple exercise to Mark, he felt inhibited. Once he practiced it, however, it became the quickest and easiest way to transform an oncoming "downer" mood into a laugh and emotional release.

Another means to release pent-up rage is pounding a pillow. Close the door to your bedroom and use a strong and durable bolster or the mattress on the bed to pound angrily with your fists and arms until you feel your anger has been fully released. If you want to, you can visualize the face of the other person in your conflict on the pillow or mattress. Rage, which includes the intention to destroy, must be appropriately discharged. As long as you remember that you will not act out your rage on actual people, this exercise can cause them no damage. In fact, in the long run it will contribute to their well-being as well as yours.

Most of us have suppressed screams of rage, especially toward our parents. Mark and Laura were raised like the rest of us with the notion that people should never raise their voices, but the following exercise changed their minds. In order to let the rage out, you can yell at the top of your lungs either into a cloth-covered pillow, with the car windows rolled up after driving to a deserted and remote spot, or under water in a swimming pool. Mark commented about this technique, "My throat sometimes gets a little sore, but after some good screams I feel much lighter and more in control of my anger."

Mark and Laura had success with other methods for discharging anger and avoiding debilitating depressions. Depression is in part anger turned inward and not released. Jogging, brisk walking, aerobic dancing, jazzercise, disco, punching a bag, swimming, competitive sports and other forms of exercise are additional enjoyable ways to let off steam. Mark and Laura always remembered to get in a morning jog to start each day refreshed, especially during their visit with his parents.

As you channel your anger and rage into positive energy through these techniques, you will likely

—Feel more loving toward family, spouse and children.

—Reduce or eliminate stress symptoms, including back, neck and stomach tensions.

—Experience more sexual vitality.

—Reduce feelings of depression and the desire to escape into drugs, alcohol or binge eating.

—Enjoy greater creativity and spontaneity.

Favoring the Positive

In childhood your parents were the ones in charge, and in most families this situation carries over into adulthood. Family get-togethers are often initiated by parents' needs, obligations and values. Rather than enjoying the times together, most younger family members reluctantly show up because they feel they "ought" to be together.

By becoming responsible for your own happiness and wanting to share your best (not your worst) with your parents, you now have the opportunity to create far more enjoyable family get-togethers. Rather than being dragged into seeing them or walking in with a chip on your shoulder, making peace with your parents frees the energy to make your relationship satisfying.

Here are ideas from some of my clients who took the initiative to improve the quality of their get-togethers with their parents:

—Instead of one person doing all the work for dinners and holidays, the "new" family tradition became potluck dinners and shared responsibilities. Each year family members alternated hosting the festivities.

—Rather than restricting their relationship with their parents to holiday dinners and stay-at-home activities, many clients began to include their parents in a variety of enjoyable activities—picnics, trips to amusement parks, symphony concerts, volunteer activities and sporting events.

—Gifts were no longer compulsively limited to birthdays and holidays. In the words of one client, "I love surprising my parents with outrageous presents when they least expect it. Last week I bought my mother a one-hour massage at a health spa. She's never had one and I thought it was about time she indulged herself with a little relaxation and pampering."

FOCUSING ON WHAT WORKS

I have noticed that some people confuse making peace with their parents with bending over backward to please them. You do not have to be controlled by the approval trap. From now on your choice is to creatively develop solutions that satisfy their needs *and* your needs. For instance, many people make the mistake of assuming that certain family traditions are sacrosanct rules that cannot be broken. As Mark and Laura demonstrated, the obligation to attend a Christmas get-together where one or both of them would be severely uncomfortable was to be avoided until the situation improved. In other cases, clients have learned to set limits with their parents so that get-togethers could be enjoyable occasions, with a minimum of unwanted obligations.

Another frequent issue arises when we ask advice from our parents when the answer they will give is obvious. For instance, if you know your parents are going to disapprove of or forbid something you desire—marrying someone they would not choose for you, pursuing a career other than the one they prefer, or making a major purchase they would discourage—*you are not obligated to ask for their opinion.* The less you need their approval and are simply willing to let them have their different point of view, the more you can be self-reliant and avoid unnecessary disputes.

Once they start getting along with their parents, some people mistakenly feel the need to "confess everything," regardless of how inappropriate that may be. After twelve years of not speaking with her mother, one woman decided to tell her mother, a devout Roman Catholic, about an affair and abortion she had had. Her mother was horrified and a new series of conflicts ensued. For months afterward, both women were emotionally upset as a result of the disclosure. Clearly, "confessing everything," when it includes incidents that your parents cannot handle, can be more harmful than helpful. You are an adult now and have a right to be private and appropriately discreet.

ACKNOWLEDGMENT IS A KEY

Some people fear that once they make peace and stop fighting with their parents, they will have nothing left to talk about! First of all, you have to remember that problems, challenges and anger will still come up in your relationship. The difference now is that you will have skills for channeling your anger effectively. Second, you need to recall your intention to share your love with your parents. Time and again I have seen that even more painful to ourselves than suppressed resentment is suppressed love. You can break through years of negativity and interpersonal conflict in your family by initiating and encouraging the following types of verbal acknowledgments:

—Tell your mother when she says something insightful, when she is being more sensitive to your needs.

—Tell your father some of the ways he has taught you to attain your goals and to achieve mastery in life.

—Give your brothers and sisters the support and encouragement you always wanted when you faced difficult challenges.

—Don't be afraid to say "I love you," no matter how many times you have suppressed those words in the past. Send flowers or a love note when they are least expected. Don't wait for anyone else to take the first step. It may feel new and risky, but the rewards for being open with your positive feelings are enormous.

—Recognize that we all need love from one another— simply because it feels good to be appreciated. Make eye contact, extend a hand or offer someone in your family a hug. Be willing to initiate a hug from your side instead of waiting for your parent to do it. Resentments may have built up in the first place because of a failure to love and be loved. Now it is up to you to bring in more love. You may have to initiate the first two hundred hugs. Remember, you are powerful and no longer need be afraid to share your love.

—Most people complain that their parents are always criticizing them when in fact *they* are always criticizing their parents, including criticizing their parents for criticizing them! Learning to break these bad habits means telling your parents what they do *right* as well as when they irritate you. When acknowledging your mother or father, be specific. Tell them with both words and facial expressions how good you feel. When they do something special for your children, be sure your parents feel appreciated. Shifting your perspective from what they do wrong to what they are doing right can open up a whole new area of things you can talk about.

—When you do or say something loving to one or both of your parents, don't be surprised if he or she has some trouble taking it in. Just as you may have felt unloved at times, they also have been acknowledged too infrequently or with too many strings attached. Give your parent a few moments to really take in the loving things you say or do. Part of saying "Thanks," "I appreciate you" and "I love you" is waiting patiently for your parents to realize just how much you appreciate them. Even if they don't get the message the first time, you must be willing to tell them again and again that your love is sincere.

4

Martyrs, Dictators and Other "Difficult" Parents

The word *peace* in the title *Making Peace with Your Parents* suggests that a war has been raging. Sometimes this struggle is between you and your actual parents. Most of the time it is an internal conflict between you and the parents you carry inside your head. This chapter will help you deal with martyrs, dictators and other difficult parents in order to gain emotional freedom and improve even the most strained relationship with your mother or father.

Parenting is never easy. In the process of wanting to influence, guide and protect their children, parents may, habitually or only at times, resort to a variety of emotional weapons that have negative psychological consequences. The most common emotional weapons, guilt and intimidation, can have long-term effects on your health and well-being as well as seriously undermining your efforts to make peace with your parents.

Guilt and Your Martyr Parent

The Martyr Mom or Dad maintains control by making you feel inappropriately responsible for your parent's suffering. With cries, sulks, health complaints and an attitude of apparent unselfishness that borders on masochism, your martyr parent can make you feel guilty for much of what you do or want that is in conflict with his or her wishes. For instance, after your martyr parent does you a favor, you might hear "Look at what I do for you." If, on the other hand, you defy your martyr parent and refuse the apparent favor, you hear "After all I've done for you, you don't even appreciate me. That's gratitude for you."

Whenever your martyr parent wants to control you, he or she simply moans, "You don't care about anyone but yourself. You're so selfish." The persistent implication is "If you loved me, you'd do what I say."

Among the guilt-inspiring comments you may have heard are:

"I gave up everything for you and this is how you thank me, like a slap in the face."

"The birth was so painful, the doctors didn't think I [your mother] was going to make it."

"I wanted you to have all the things I never had, but look at you now . . . you don't even care."

"The only reason we stayed together was because of you."

"So you're going on vacation and not coming to visit? Have a nice time."

"Of course you're very busy and you don't have time to call. I understand perfectly."

The underlying message you receive from your Martyr Mom or Dad is that being who you are hurts your parent. This can lead to a pervasive sense of guilt in your life. To illustrate how you may feel trapped or manipulated by a martyr parent, see from your own experience if you can recognize any of the following conflicting messages:

"You're an adult now and you have your own life to live . . . But how come you never want to visit anymore?"

"I only want you to be happy . . . But for once in your life can't you stop being so selfish and think about how I feel?"

"It's your decision and no one can make it for you . . . But if you'd listen to me, these problems would never happen."

"Of course you're entitled to your own values [lifestyle, friends, religious beliefs, etc.] . . . But I have to ask myself, 'Where did we go wrong?' "

If these are accompanied by enough groans and sighs, you are left feeling guilty and immobilized.

Intimidation and Your Dictator Parent

With a somewhat different style, the Dictator Dad or Mom regularly uses fear and intimidation to get you to obey his or her wishes. When you cross the dictator parent, you hear an angry outburst that roars, "You lazy, no-good, rotten, ungrateful kid. You do what I say or else I'll punish you like you'll never forget." With an ever-present threat of physical or emotional violence, your dictator parent has terrified you with the sneer, the look of contempt, the pointing finger or the beet-red glare that makes you tremble with fear that he or she is about to explode. Just as the martyr parent says, in effect, "Look at what you're doing to me," the dictator parent says, in effect, "Look what I'm going to do to you."

Fear-inducing statements your dictator parent may have used to get you to obey or to belittle you include

> "How could you be so stupid? I told you not to do that!"
> "I don't care how old [educated, rich, famous] you are. I'm still your parent and I know what I'm talking about."
> "Don't lie to me. What are you really doing with those lousy [strange, weird, slovenly] friends of yours?"
> "If you ever raise your voice to me again, I'll smack you so hard it'll make your head spin."
> "I don't have to explain anything. You'll do it because I say so. Period!"
> "While I'm paying the bills, I'm the boss."

Like the martyr parent, the bottom line with the dictator parent is control: "If you're good, you'll do as I say." Using anger, a raised voice or bullying tactics to control you, your dictator parent intimidates you one moment and then demands your affection the next by saying

> "Don't be so sensitive."
> "Can't you take a joke?"
> "You know I'm only doing what's best for you."
> "Next time think first and this won't happen again."

No wonder you have been burning up inside every time an authority figure tries to control or bully you. Even though you're no longer under the physical domination of your parents, you still may be intimidated by their or anyone else's anger.

Inner Conflict

Even if it has been years since you heard your martyr parent moan and say "Do whatever you want. Why should you care how I feel?" or since you have been attacked by a dictator parent's violent rage, the memories and negative feelings are still present. Frequently *the offspring of a martyr or a dictator internalize the guilt and intimidation so well that they tend to pressure, punish and control themselves with far more vehemence than their parents ever did!* If you are a self-criticizing person or often feel "no matter what I do it's never enough," then the struggle you face is not only with your actual parent but, perhaps more important, with yourself as well.

Your "difficult" parent may alternate between martyr *and* dictator, acting hurt and self-denying one moment while raging angrily the next. In some cases, these coercive styles are made even more troublesome by the added problems of divorce, alcoholism, drug addiction or emotional instability. Regardless of what type of difficulties your parents had and whether or not one or both is a martyr, a dictator or a combination of the two, you should recognize that like many children, *you may have consciously or unconsciously felt responsible for your parents' problems.* When something bad happens to a parent, quite often the child feels guilty. When a parent is chronically anxious, depressed or angry, the child may feel responsible. When parents divorce, the children are often left wondering whether it was their fault. When a parent is troubled by alcohol, drugs, financial setbacks, illness or emotional problems, the child often asks, "What did I do that caused the pain?"

"Driving Each Other Crazy"

A thirty-year-old social worker, Julie was a client who grew up feeling responsible for her parents' problems. Overworked and underpaid, she came to our health center with a classic case of "burnout." No matter how much she was told she needed rest and more enjoyment in her life, Julie had continued to work long hours and put everyone else's needs ahead of her own. As a consequence, she frequently came down with a bad cold, flu, bronchitis or some other illness.

As a result of her training as a social worker, Julie showed an awareness of the dynamics in her family. Her Martyr Mom was a highly intelligent woman who had quit her job as a newspaper reporter in order to have children. She resented being married to Julie's father, a cold and rarely available workaholic who ran a chain of sporting-goods stores with outlets spread over a five-state region.

According to Julie, "The hostility in my family was so thick you could cut it with a knife. Even though they rarely fought, the tension was always there. Most of the time it came out in little snips of anger. My dad would say something like 'When I drop dead you'll finally appreciate how much I sacrifice for you and the family.' Mom would snap back, 'Then at least I'll have an excuse for why you're never home.' "

Her training as a social worker aside, Julie still had frequent troubles whenever she visited her parents. Because it was a long trip to her parents' home, Julie would stay with them for a week or two at a time. Yet after three days under the same roof, she and her mother were "driving each other crazy." Julie told me, "No matter what I do she finds fault. And each time I feel like a criminal because she gets so hurt and upset. All I have to do is misplace the salt shaker and you'd think I'd dealt her a mortal blow."

When she's not with them, Julie's parents call nearly every Sunday. "The conversations start out fine. I tell them what's new and how the weather is. But then they start in on who's sick, who died, who got married, who got divorced and which of my old friends did something that upset their parents. The message each week is essentially that 'nothing's new. We hate our lives. No one cares. Kids are ungrateful. If you cared and visited more often, we wouldn't be suffering as much as we are.' "

Two months before Julie came to me for therapy, her mother called and woke her at 7:00 A.M.

"What's wrong?" Julie asked.

"Nothing's wrong," her mother snapped. "Since when is it a crime for a mother to call her own daughter?"

"Mom, it's seven in the morning."

"I thought you had to get up for work. I'm sorry. I only called to tell you I'm coming out to see you."

"Terrific! When?"

"Your father's going to be away starting next week. I don't want to be alone."

"How long are you going to stay?"

"What's the matter? You don't want me there, do you?"

"Mom, I didn't say that."

"But that's what you meant. All right, I won't come."

Julie found herself apologizing profusely and agreeing to

let her mother come and stay for two weeks at Julie's apartment while her father opened a new store in another state. The visit was traumatic, with Julie's mother repeatedly criticizing her cooking, clothes, boyfriends, furnishings, health habits and lifestyle in general. Whenever Julie tried to defend herself, her mother brooded silently and offered, "I'll go back and stay in that empty house alone. At least then I won't be hated by my own daughter." After missing most of the next three weeks of work because of a bad case of the flu, Julie made an appointment to see me.

Playing Rescuer or Victim

Like that of many children of martyr parents, Julie's behavior alternated between two ineffective roles: rescuer and victim. Over the years she had attempted to become her mother's friend, therapist, adviser and even adopted parent. In her role as rescuer, Julie quite often found herself caught in the middle between her mother and father when the two of them were having an argument. As though it were Julie's responsibility to be the peacemaker in the family, she felt compelled to get involved every time one or both of her parents were upset or unhappy. She could even see how her choosing a career as a social worker was another way of trying to learn the skills and insights to handle family crises, including the one in her own family.

Yet she was unable to recognize how being a rescuer and trying to save her Martyr Mom often made Julie herself feel and act like a victim and fellow martyr. She wanted to believe that she could heal the rifts and longstanding conflicts between her parents. She was convinced that if only her mother would listen, she would no longer suffer. She was determined to be the miracle-worker who made everyone in her family happy and secure. Twenty-four hours a day it was Julie to the rescue!

Julie did not succeed in changing the situation; in fact her inability to say "No" to her mother made her feel resentful and blame the very person she thought she wanted to help. Her unwillingness to care for her own health properly was taking its toll. Her refusal to set aside more time for nurturing and enjoying herself also became a way of trying to "outbleed" her mother.

It was as though Julie were responding to her mother's lament of "Look what you're doing to me" with her own lament, "But look what you (and everyone else) are doing to *me.*" By refusing to express her needs, set limits and care for her own health and well-being, Julie was falling victim to the same martyr syndrome she disliked so much in her mother.

Cutting the Emotional Umbilical Cord

As with most children of martyr parents, Julie was reluctant or unable to feel at peace with herself while her mother was suffering. Whenever her mother cried out in misery or made a guilt-inducing statement, Julie immediately reacted by feeling guilty, self-critical, depressed or unsure of whether she had a right to enjoy her life. I explained to Julie: "The goal is not to fight, beg, run from or become just like your mother. You don't have to be controlled by her depression and unhappiness, nor can you change her. Assume that she won't change. Instead, your goal is to modify your emotional response so that *you* can choose an appropriate and effective reaction."

The victim in us always complains, "But my parent is *making* me feel guilty—he or she is doing it to me." To become accountable for your own feelings, you need to be able to say, "How and why do I choose to feel guilty? What can I do instead that will support me as well as my martyr parent more effectively?" Guilt is not something your parent does to you. As I told Julie, "Your mom does what she does and then you choose to react with guilt and to attempt to rescue her; then you feel angry, disappointed and victimized because you can't change her."

For anyone who grew up with a martyr parent, it is essential to recognize that *guilt is self-punishment you don't deserve.* In truth, Julie had neither caused nor could remedy her mother's emotional distress. To illustrate how guilt operates and to help Julie stop blaming herself for her mother's self-critical and self-destructive habits, I stood up in the middle of one of our sessions and walked to the window.

"Now, if I jumped out this window head-first and splattered myself on the pavement below, killing or crippling myself, would it be your fault?"

Julie laughed and said, "Of course not."

"But what if I left behind a note that described how Julie looked at me the wrong way, that Julie only thinks about herself, or that Julie wasn't living up to my expectations of progress in psychotherapy? Then would it be your fault?"

Julie hesitated for a moment before she replied, "No, it would still be ridiculous. I'm not the one who made you jump."

I asked her to consider how that "note" was essentially the same control device Julie had allowed her mother to use on her for years. When she saw the connection, Julie's face lit up. She admitted, "For a second there I almost thought I was to blame for you jumping out the window." Julie realized that she had a choice of whether or not to feel guilty. When responding to her Martyr Mom or anyone else, she had more options than simply the roles of rescuer or victim. She now had the necessary insight to cut the emotional umbilical cord.

Defusing the Guilt

Even though you may not like the guilt-inducing statements and behavior perpetrated by your martyr parent, you do *not* have to react automatically like an out-of-control stimulus-response machine. When he or she says "Jump," you do not have to jump or feel guilty. When your parent implies "Either do what I say or you'll hurt me," you do not have to bend over backward to try to please him or her (injuring yourself in the process).

Three weeks before Julie was scheduled to fly back home to be with her family at her cousin's wedding, I asked her to do a guilt desensitization exercise that has helped thousands of clients defuse their automatic guilt response and deal more effectively with a martyr parent. Instead of being forced to feel resentful and wanting to fight or flee every time your martyr parent tries to make you feel guilty, you can learn to stop, relax and choose a more appropriate response. By handling the "difficult" behavior without getting hurt, enraged or feeling trapped, you will no longer be at the mercy of your Martyr Mom or Dad.

The exercise requires that you begin by making a list of at least five of the most common guilt-inducing lines or situations your martyr parent uses or has used. By defusing your response to the most common guilt-inducing phrases, you will also become more effective in handling other statements and behavior that may catch you by surprise. Since we learn best from specifics, from which we then can generalize, be sure to make your list of guilt-inducing statements as realistic as possible. The more your lines sound exactly like those of your martyr parent, the more guilt-defusing and healing can take place.

The list Julie made of the five most guilt-inducing statements her mother tended to deliver were as follows:

"So when are you getting married? You know that none of us is getting any younger."

"You used to be such a sweet girl. I don't know what happened. But it's no wonder you're not married—you probably scare all the men away."

"Is that what they're wearing these days? I was so embarrassed in front of my friends."

"I was sick the entire week, but I didn't want to bother you. I know how busy you are."

"I hope that when you have children they don't grow up as ungrateful as mine."

Once you have compiled your list of guilt-inducing statements, either record it on a tape machine exactly as your parent would say it or ask a close friend, lover or spouse to read the list to you with the proper intonation and emphasis. The first few times that you hear your list of guilt-inducing statements, you may need to release some anger at your martyr parent. Frequently, guilt is anger turned inward. As you begin to see how much you have been controlled by these messages, hurt and frustration are bound to result. Now is an opportunity to release the rage your guilt has been covering up.

Take some time to vent your anger safely and appropriately. Pound a mattress, scream into a pillow or hit a punching bag until you feel the anger subside. If you feel exhausted from this emotional discharge, be sure to take ten or fifteen minutes to rest and regain your calm. After you have released your anger a number of times, you will be ready to take the next step in the exercise.

Giving Yourself Some Peace

In this guilt desensitization technique, you will go behind the hurt and anger. Underneath the rage, there may be sadness and tears. Covered up by the pain of holding back your suppressed feelings is a core of love, joy and inner peace.

Unplug the phones, put a "Do Not Disturb" sign on the door, find a comfortable chair and have your tape recorder or friend ready at your side. Close your eyes and take five very slow, deep breaths, exhaling through your mouth. Begin to notice the soothing effects of settling down. Direct your attention to your toes and feel them relax. Let your attention slowly glide up your body—feet, ankles, calves, knees, thighs, hips, abdomen, back, chest, neck, hands, arms, face —and stop at each part to feel relaxation taking place.

Now imagine that you are floating in space or lying in a warm meadow. Create any mental image that you find peaceful, relaxing and enjoyable. Let the world slip away and drift naturally in your reveries. From this safe and relaxed place within, you can perceive yourself without self-criticism. You can feel the release of letting down your defenses. As you progress in your relaxation, you can feel the love and inner peace that are deep inside you.

When you are feeling relaxed and comfortable, turn on the tape recording or signal your friend that you are ready. Continue to experience the relaxed and peaceful feelings as you listen once again to your list of guilt-inducing statements. With each statement, picture your parent as realistically as possible. Observe your feelings and thoughts as they arise. After each statement, stop and rest for a moment while continuing to relax, unwind and breathe slowly and comfortably.

As you listen to the statements a number of times, you may experience some tension in your chest, shoulders or neck. Your breathing may become shallow or feel constricted. Without resisting the feelings and sensations as they arise, continue to focus your attention on the peaceful images you created in the relaxation exercise. Remember to breathe slowly and comfortably, letting go of any tension. Continue to relax, unwind and feel comfortable. The goal of this exercise is to remain clear-headed and at peace even when you are confronted by guilt-inducing statements. Only after you have heard each statement at least three or four times and have continued to feel relaxed should you then slowly open your eyes and return your attention to reality. It is helpful to repeat this exercise a number of times, especially before a visit with your parents.

You may at times fall back into old patterns and feel yourself starting to react automatically to one of your martyr parent's guilt-inducing statements. During those moments, remember to stop, relax and choose a more appropriate response. By breathing slowly and recalling the warmth and relaxation you achieved in this exercise, you will be more likely to deal effectively with your martyr parent. When you "blow it" and find yourself erupting, you can repeat the exercise. Retraining emotional habits isn't easy, but with patience and practice comes expertise. Remember that instead of blaming your parent and feeling victimized, you have skills to retain your equanimity even when confronted by guilt-inducing comments. You now have two choices— one is to react blindly, the other is to stop, relax and choose.

Your Parent's Inner Child

Once you defuse the guilt responses that used to "drive you crazy," you can take another valuable step in making peace with even the most difficult martyr parent. Within each of us, no matter how adult we may think or act, is an inner child who still carries unresolved hurts, needs and demands. In the case of your martyr parent, that inner child is a powerful and insistent force that not only controls the moods and behavior of your parent but also tries to control and manipulate you with its guilt-inducing devices. Unless you are able to understand and be supportive of your parent's inner child, you will still be fighting a painful war you cannot win.

Part of making peace with your martyr parent may be learning to appreciate the traditions, religion, national origin, family conflicts and childhood traumas that make your parent the way he or she is. It may be important to ask about and understand the social, political and economic forces (such as what it was like emigrating to another country, what it was like during the Great Depression, what it was like growing up with various hardships) that affected your parent.

The exercise I recommend to clients is a visualization

technique that you can do prior to a visit or phone call, or whenever you are feeling put-upon or threatened by a martyr parent. All you need is a photograph of your parent when he or she was a young child. If you are unable to locate an old photograph, any of your memories of having seen old photos or having imagined your parent as a young child will suffice. In addition, you can get information, stories and insights from aunts, uncles, cousins or others who knew your parent as a child.

Begin by looking at the image of your parent as a child. What was he or she feeling then? What insecurities and pressures were controlling that small child? What was she taught about how she should be as a woman, wife and mother? What was he taught about how he should be as a man, husband and father? How does that inner child feel about itself? What unresolved conflicts are affecting its moods?

It can be especially helpful if you locate a photo in which your parent is shown as a child or adolescent with his or her parents, brothers and sisters. What can you discover about the inner conflicts and unresolved needs of your parent by examining how he or she fit into that family situation? Were your grandparents stern or loving? Look at the expressions on their faces, the way they sit or stand, the body language that is visible in the photographs. What pressures were put on your parent's shoulders? What were the relationships like between your parent and his or her brothers and sisters? Were they competitive, supportive, loving or cold? What losses and deaths in the family have affected your parent since that photograph was taken?

Look closely at how your parent relates to others in the photographs. Is he or she playful or distant? Proud or shy?

Relaxed or stiff? Smiling happily or awkwardly, because the photographer said to? Is he or she alone or making contact with others? If you can find a wedding or honeymoon photo of your parents, notice how they seem to be relating. What hopes and dreams were in their minds when that picture was taken? What struggles and losses have they faced in the years since? Can you find a sensitive, warm, loving and needy person in these or other photographs? If so, you will improve your ability to relate to your difficult parent regardless of how he or she acts today.

Caution: It is important not to move too quickly to understanding your parent's inner child or forgiving your parent. This exercise should come *after* you have released your resentments, ventilated your anger and defused your guilt. If you use your insight and understanding to invalidate or preempt your anger, you may wind up feeling emotionally stuck and guilty. However, if you learn to understand and support your parent's inner child *after* having worked through your anger and upsets, you will be far more likely to be forgiving and relaxed when you are with your martyr parent.

As Julie discovered about her own mother, most martyr parents felt like victims and used guilt-inducing statements to get attention long before they became parents. In most cases *the difficult incidents and disappointments have little, if anything, to do with what you have done or said as that martyr parent's child.* You will discover by visualizing your parent as a child or by talking to your parent's relatives and friends that his or her suffering had earlier antecedents and that this suffering was later projected onto you.

A week before her trip to attend her cousin's wedding, Julie spent an hour on the phone with her mother's sister and then brought old photographs of her mother to my office to do the visualization exercise. As she related what her aunt had told her, Julie's eyes filled with tears.

"It's no accident that my mother is always worried that I'm going to abandon her. When she was seven, her parents were divorced and she only saw her father a few times before he died. I can see why she gets so hurt and resentful whenever my father leaves home on one of his extended business trips. She's still essentially that abandoned little girl who can't understand why her parents are no longer together."

Even though Julie felt empathy for her mother's pain, she also saw that the roots of her mother's unhappiness were neither caused nor could be remedied by Julie's actions. In addition, Julie realized that her mother was constantly beating herself up emotionally. The guilt-inducing "you're not enough" comments her mother made to Julie once in a while were made to herself repeatedly.

I explained to Julie that no matter how much she might want her mother to change, she must give up the fantasy. "As much as you might try, you can never make up for what she didn't get as a child. The more you try, the more you will be frustrated, because you cannot undo what's already been done."

As I suggested to Julie, the greatest contribution you can make to yourself and your martyr parent is to take care of yourself and enjoy your life. By defusing your guilt and understanding that you cannot take away the pain experienced by your parent's inner child, you will then be free to give your mom or dad what underneath it all a parent really wants—your happiness and love. Instead of sacrificing yourself and resenting your parent, you will have the peace of mind necessary to accept your parent as he or she is. Instead of fearing your parent's inner child and resisting its demands for attention, you can simply be reassuring that he or she is special, important, loved and understood. This does not mean becoming patronizing, belittling or self-righteous with your parent. Having empathy for your parent's inner child is an exercise to help you understand your parent better and to deal with him or her more effectively.

For years I had noticed that my own mother felt hurt, neglected and unsure of herself as a parent whenever I didn't follow her advice or way of doing things. Because of the insecure feelings of her inner child, we engaged in regular battles in which her statements and behavior implied "If you love me, you'll do as I say." When I later learned to firmly but gently say, "Mom, I want you to know that I love you even when I don't do exactly as you say," it was like a revelation to her. Breaking free of the approval trap was as much a gift to her peace of mind as it was to mine. Our parents don't want our sacrifice so much as they want our love. They want us to know that they are loving us *the best way they know how,* given what their life experiences have been. Don't forget, they had parents too!

Avoiding Getting Caught in the Melodrama

In the past, your reactions to your martyr parent were automatic—fight or flight, rescuer or victim. Now that you have learned to defuse your guilt, you have a choice of how to respond. You can get caught up in the melodrama *or* you can continue to feel relaxed and comfortable even when your parent is trying to control you with guilt. While staying calm when your martyr parent cries out in pain may feel to you like indifference or "not caring," it is quite the opposite. As

I stated earlier, psychological growth involves the integration of seemingly conflicting values. Not getting caught up in your martyr parent's cries for help allows you to have compassion, to choose an appropriate response and to stop feeling guilty, resentful and victimized. By maintaining your equanimity, you can be more effective and also avoid contributing to further upsets.

To make lasting changes in your relationship with your martyr parent, you may have to develop a more positive identity of your own and give up your role as part of his or her melodrama. If your parents continue to fight and argue with each other, you may choose not to play the referee who always gets caught in the middle. If your parents are constantly sad or depressed, you may choose not to play the clown who feels obligated to cheer them up. If your parents often suffer from psychosomatic symptoms, you may choose not to be the twenty-four-hour-a-day nurse. Your responsibility is to love your parents, not to become their adopted parent and best friend, especially if it means sacrificing your own health and well-being.

While it may be difficult at times to let go of the melodrama that has persisted in your family, you must recognize that the roles that helped you survive in the past may no longer be serving you now. If you notice that you are caught in guilt or in established patterns of behavior that you no longer need or want, don't be critical of yourself. Simply recognize how you could have better handled the situation and remember to stop, relax and choose a more appropriate response next time.

During her visit to attend her cousin's wedding and see her parents, Julie wrote me the following letter, which illustrates how she avoided getting caught up in her mother's melo-drama:

Dear Dr. Bloomfield,

Hi! I decided to stay with my sister and her husband this time. In addition to the wedding, I've seen my parents three times for limited periods—a lunch, a movie and a party at my cousin's house. I'm happy to say that this visit has been very different from all the others. Not that there weren't times when I wanted to scream, but this time I was much more relaxed and actually en-joyed seeing my mom and dad.

The one time I almost lost it, though, was when we were having lunch and Mom said, "Are you still seeing Chris?" I think I told you that they're worried sick that I'm going to marry Chris and he's not Jewish.

I started to feel guilty and was almost ready to yell "It's none of your business" and storm out of the restaurant, which I had done in the past. Instead, I leaned back, took a few breaths and looked across the table. Calmly but assertively, I said, "Mom, you know I love you even when I don't do everything you approve of. Chris and I are doing fine and he sends his best."

It was great. I had no need to justify or defend myself. I realized that she can't make me do anything anymore. My mother is enti-tled to her values, opinions and upsets. If she would prefer that I not marry someone who isn't Jewish, I can accept that she feels that way. After all, she doesn't have to conform to my expectations either!

Looking back on the trip, I don't think *they* were very different this visit than usual. They argued and complained a lot and it was hard at times seeing how much they beat themselves up over nothing. But even if they never change, I can still give them a lot more love and not feel manipulated. This is the first trip home where I didn't wind up with a headache or a nervous stomach.

I'll call you when I get back in town.

With love,
Julie

Playing Meek or Defiant

While the martyr parent used guilt to control you, the dictator parent used fear and intimidation to keep you in line or simply to vent his or her rage upon you. Having grown up with a parent who was habitually short-tempered, belittling, insensitive or authoritarian, you may have acquired an internal voice that is even more intimidating and controlling than your father or mother ever was. Toward all authority figures, this internal critic says, "Do what they say *or else.* You'll get your revenge later." As a result, your behavior may fluctuate between playing meek and playing defiant, neither of which is now an effective way to deal with fear and intimidation.

By suppressing their anger and internalizing their parent's belittling criticisms and threats, the children of a dictator parent often suffer from excessive anxiety, rebelliousness or self-destructive habits. As a result of having to deal with a Dictator Dad or Mom, you may notice yourself

—Wanting to walk out of projects, jobs and relationships with defiant anger.

—Stopping short of your goals and dreams, as if to say, vengefully, "You were right. I am a worthless nobody."

—Defiantly engaging in overeating, smoking, or alcohol or drug abuse, as if to say "See what you did to me."

—Finding yourself with a boss, a spouse and friends who belittle you the way your dictator parent did.

—Taking out your suppressed anger on your spouse and children.

—Holding the anger inside you until you either explode or find yourself ill.

—Hiding your own strengths and power by being overly

weak, "nice" and compliant so that no one will notice or criticize you.

—Being excessively self-critical; thinking of yourself as "lazy," "stupid" or "ugly."

—Always being hungry for approval, even from people who don't matter to you or who are unlikely to give it.

Regardless of how strongly you may want to avoid, ignore or get back at your dictator parent, an important step in breaking free of such symptoms and behavior patterns is making peace with even the most difficult dictator father or mother. Mary, a client of mine, has had an enormous challenge in dealing with her fiery father, who on the one hand was a good provider and on the other hand could be insensitive and even violent to his wife and children. In order to benefit most from how she made peace with an uncommunicative and authoritarian Dictator Dad, I asked Mary to tell her own story.

"I'll Teach You a Lesson You'll Never Forget"

"My earliest memory was when I was awakened in the middle of the night by screams and banging in the kitchen. I was three years old. As I ran into the hall, I saw my father holding a large kitchen knife in one hand. He had my mother by the hair in the other hand. She was sobbing and yelling, 'Jack, please don't.' His eyes were filled with rage as he said, 'You bitch, you deserve it.' I remember calling out something and he saw me and hollered, 'Get out of here!'

"In my family there were five brothers and sisters. At least three times a month there were violent fights where my mother would come out of her room with black eyes and bruises all over her. One time the children huddled together in one room crying and my older brother said, 'I'm going to get back at him some day.' I said, 'I hate his guts . . . I wish he was dead,' and my sister said, 'Let's all run away and never come back.'

"One time he came home in the middle of the night with his friends and woke me up, saying, 'Get out there and help your mother make some food for me and my friends.' Without saying a word, she and I proceeded to cook a full-course meal. Needless to say, as I grew into my teen years, he started to show the same jealousy and protectiveness toward me that he did with my mother. My mother supported me in a dancing and acting career, but he never did. Instead, when I was asked to do a film, his reaction was, 'You're not doing that . . . all actresses are whores. Is that what you are?'

"During those early teen years, every time I came home from somewhere he would look at me suspiciously and say, 'You slut, I know what you've been doing.' I remember feeling very confused and angry. One night he was beating my mother and I couldn't stand it any longer. I went up to him and said, 'You don't love anyone but yourself. You're selfish and mean and I hate you!' He grabbed the bedpost, ripped it off and started beating me with it, saying, 'I'm going to teach you a lesson you'll never forget.' I ran away and hid in the bushes. From that time on my plan was to leave home as soon as I could.

"At fifteen I became pregnant and was completely rejected by my father. His friends would come over and he told my mother to tell me to hide in my room until they left. When I was three months pregnant and barely showing, he told my mother to send me away somewhere. Feeling helpless and afraid, she took me to a home for unwed mothers and left me there for six months with no money, no books to read and no nice clothes. She was instructed to give me nothing, even though they were very wealthy. I remember visiting at home after I had had the baby and it was given up for adoption. My father would leave the room when I walked in—complete rejection, and not one word was said. It was obvious from his facial expressions, though, that he felt rage and hostility toward me.

"From that time on, I would visit and stay for short periods. It was always my intention to somehow communicate with my father and find some meeting ground. The many attempts I made were unsuccessful. He became more defensive and intimidating, and I would say to myself, 'Forget it, he's not ready yet.' I asked him for money to pay for my business college and he said, 'You think I'm made of money —business college is a joke, it won't do you any good.' Then he threw the money at me. At that point in our relationship, I was unable to feel any love or understanding for him. I felt misunderstood and abandoned. If I were to go to him and ask for help, I was sure he'd reject me."

Changing Perspective

For the next twelve years, Mary lived away from her parents. Though she rarely visited them, she continued to stay in contact with her mother. She wanted to resolve the problems with her father—to understand the "inner child" within him. Locating an old photograph of her father and his family, Mary called her mother, described the photograph and began to ask questions about why her father acted the way he did. What were his parents like? Why did Mary's mother stay with him? Why did she still love him and take care of him? Instead of closing her mind to any positive sides about her father or trying to change her mother's feelings of love for him, Mary gradually began to uncover the pressures and influences that had made her father into a Dictator Dad.

Mary learned that her father had been saddled with tremendous pressures and responsibilities as a result of being the first-born male. His mother, a very powerful and intimidating woman, never let up telling him what to do and how to do it. When Mary's parents were first married, her father's mother used to insist that he eat her cooking instead of his wife's because "your wife isn't Catholic . . . she's not good enough to take care of you." As Mary's father began to take on more aggressive characteristics and became successful in business, he repeatedly had to face the belittling criticisms and controlling devices of his mother. No matter what he did to support and help his younger brothers and sisters, he was always told it wasn't enough.

Even though Mary grew up perceiving her father as a powerful authority figure, her mother's stories helped her discover that underneath the gruff exterior, her father was an insecure and self-critical person who had never made peace with *his* dictator parent. In most cases, my clients with a dictator parent have found that their parent had a need to be authoritarian and belittling in order to cover up a fragile ego or low self-esteem. Inside most bullies, you will find an inner child who has been bullied or belittled. Instead of feeling responsible or victimized by your dictator parent's rage and insensitivity, you must recognize that the anger and hurt have nothing to do with you. Instead of internalizing the criticisms of your dictator parent and reacting with meekness or defiance, you can choose more appropriate and effective responses.

Owning Your Power

During the past few years, Mary began to work out her anger and resentments toward her father. She found that making a list of her resentments, dealing with her anger constructively, and learning to forgive her father were particularly helpful to her. She also began to experiment to find ways to make some contact with her father beyond the superficial and unsatisfying phone calls. Whenever Mary's mother would call and put Mary's father on the phone, he would say abruptly and without feeling, "Is everything O.K.? Good, here's your mother."

At first Mary tried to reach her father by writing a long letter in which she described how much she wanted to get to know him as a person and to break through their differences. She never received a reply. Then she tried initiating some phone calls to her father. Each time, though, he would cut them short and give the phone to her mother.

In spite of the frustration she felt with each attempt to make contact with her father, Mary knew it was still something she wanted to achieve. Yet she also realized that each time she wrote, called or talked to him, she remained intimidated and afraid, as though he were an all-powerful giant. Even though she was now an adult, she still felt inside like a frightened child facing a man whom she perceived as much stronger and more threatening than was actually the case.

When she was feeling especially powerless, Mary and I did a role-playing exercise that has been successful with many people who view themselves as intimidated by their dictator parent. This exercise can be done alone or with a close friend.

It simply requires a willingness to role-play and experience whatever insights come from the exercise.

I asked Mary to sit on the floor and look up while I stood on top of a chair and towered over her. From that vantage point, in which I was more than twice her size, Mary said she could imagine how powerless and tiny she felt when she was a small child confronted by her Dictator Dad. As I glared down at her and bellowed some of the angry and intimidating lines she had heard her father use time and again, I could see her cringing in fear as well as building up resentments and anger.

Then we switched positions so that I sat on the floor while she stood on the chair. Towering over me and shouting back at me what she wished she had said to her father, Mary for the first time felt how much power she actually had. She was no longer the helpless child dealing with a powerful giant. Now as a result of owning her power, she was free to become more assertive and effective when dealing with her father. No longer at his mercy, she could deal with him adult to adult.

Breakthrough

During her next phone call with her father, Mary told him, "Dad, I don't want to have a superficial conversation with you anymore. Before you die, I want us to have made some positive contact." After a pause, he admitted that he was confused and unsure about the strong emotions she had expressed in the long letter she had sent him a few months earlier. He also said for the first time, "I'm open to talking with you if that's what you'd like."

Yet the next time she called and said she was ready to

discuss some things that had been on her mind for years, her father said, "Not now, your mother's not home. I have to go." Mary was furious and decided to call back. She said, "Dad, the only conversation I have with you now is by phone and I feel really hurt when I call and you have no time to talk to me." As she describes the phone call, "I felt so proud that I'd overcome my feelings of intimidation. Normally I would have carried that anger around with me. This time I let him know how I felt and we ended up having a great conversation about what was really going on in our lives."

Recently, Mary went to visit her parents. It was her first visit with them in three years. As Mary tells it, "My mother had arranged a party for my husband and me. As the plane landed I started to feel anxious and excited. We arrived at the house and I walked through the group of relatives and friends, saying, 'I have to see my father first.' I suppose right up until that moment there was some lingering doubt as to whether I could really forgive him or accept him exactly as he was. Then I saw him sitting there with his big brown eyes looking my way. I went straight into his arms and cried. In those few precious moments with my father I felt cleansed of my hatred for him. Even though I did not condone the way he had treated my mother or the rest of us, I now felt compassion and understanding for him. I could feel his caring without any words. I was complete."

While most of us were fortunate not to have been exposed to physical violence when we were younger, we were nevertheless affected by the "emotional violence" and intimidation in our families. There are many ways to frighten and intimidate children besides beating them—whether your dictator parent expressed his or her rage with fists, words or threats, the effect is quite often the same.

Guilt and intimidation are used in every family. Part of growing up is making peace with the coercive means your parents used in what they thought was your best interest.

What Are Your Chances?

Every now and then I hear clients say, "I'm sure these techniques work in general, but my case is different. My 'difficult' parent is just too much." That may be true to the extent that no matter what you do or say, your "difficult" parent continues to exhibit the same behavior as before. Yet that does not mean you have been unsuccessful in making peace with your mother or father. *Changes in their behavior are not the measure of whether you are making progress.*

If you conscientiously work through your resentments, learn to express love and constructive anger, and defuse the guilt and intimidation with your "difficult" parent, *what your parent does and says will no longer have the power to control your health and well-being.* If you succeed at least as far as making peace with the parents inside your head, you will have stopped blaming them for your problems and stopped depending on them for your needs, self-respect or peace of mind. That may mean breaking free of the financial and emotional bonds that have kept you from taking care of yourself. That may mean letting go of the unrealistic expectations and demands you place on your parents long after they have stopped meeting them. For each of us, it means *no longer being a victim in our relationship with our parents.*

Most people who continue to suffer from unresolved and conflicting feelings with their parents are waiting for something that may never occur. "If only they would do or say _____, I'd forgive them." "If only they would accept me for

_____, I'd make the effort to get along with them." "If only they'd stop doing or saying _____, I'd be more accepting."

Even if your parent's alcoholism, drug addiction or emotional instability makes communication and trust difficult, you *can* make peace with that parent without requiring him or her to change. Even if one or both of your parents refuses to accept your choice of career, your choice of spouse, or your sexual identity as a gay, bisexual or lesbian, you *can* put an end to the emotional warfare by making peace with the parents inside your head. Even if your parent is unloving, unavailable or no longer alive, you *can* and must get your own emotional needs met to regain your peace of mind.

The fundamental problem in dealing with difficult or unavailable parents is not the statements or behavior that irritate you. Rather, the source of the emotional pain and psychological distance has been your inability to express the suppressed feelings of love you have for your mother and father. For Mary, Julie and thousands of others, learning how to accept and love a difficult parent took time and effort but was not impossible. In each case, the breakthrough came as the individuals learned to grow and accept their parents exactly as they are. What assisted this process was learning how to visit their parents without unrealistic expectations and to take care of their own needs for emotional support through building a "surrogate family."

Building a Surrogate Family

By "surrogate family" I mean the emotional support groups that we each need at work, with friends, in community activities and for leisure-time fun. Unless you take stock of what emotional, guidance and nurturance needs are not being met at the present time, you will continue to look to your parents for needs they are not likely to fulfill. Instead of resenting what their parents cannot give them (and no parents could ever provide for all of our needs), those who have made peace with their parents did so by building friendships and networks for support.

Even though Julie had been on her own for a number of years, she still hadn't developed a strong support network. Because her mother had repeatedly told her when she was growing up, "You shouldn't wash your dirty laundry in public—what goes on among family members is nobody's business," Julie realized that she was unable to confide her problems or ask for help, even from her friends. When her friends were planning weekend adventures or relaxing get-togethers, Julie was frequently "too busy" to join in the fun. Even though she considered herself a proponent of women's rights, Julie depended on her boyfriends for companionship and was reluctant to join the support groups and stable friendships fostered by many of the women she worked with. On an emotional level, Julie had learned not to trust anyone or let anyone in.

During the months while Julie worked through her feelings of guilt and responsibility for her mother's problems, she began to explore a number of ways to meet her needs for emotional support. Instead of viewing her co-workers as competitors, she began to let down her social defenses. She chose two close women friends whom she began to have lunch with, confide her feelings to and join for weekend day trips to nearby museums, parks and concerts. At work she began to delegate more to those who had lighter work loads.

At night she began to plan relaxing and stress-free activities that were a marked contrast to the nonstop client calls that used to fill her evenings.

As Julie explained, "The more I learned to take care of my needs, the more I stopped resenting my mother for not sharing my interests and values. As I began to enjoy my friends more, not only did my mom not get angry, but she soon began imitating me. As a result of my reaching out to others and asking for help, she's gotten a little more assertive in terms of confiding in her friends and starting an exercise program twice a week. Even though I don't try to give her advice anymore, she follows my lead more than she ever did. My clients, too, are learning to depend less on me and meet their own emotional needs. I'm letting my clients grow up. I don't have to try to save them anymore."

During the time that Mary lived apart from her parents, she nevertheless provided for her support and guidance by "adopting" parents, role models and friends who could give her the love and respect her father could not. Mary explains, "Coming from a close-knit family with five brothers and sisters, I was used to having lots of people around, lots of intimacy and close contact. When I moved away from home, I missed that much more than I missed my parents. Not too long after I moved to another city, I found another family, with a mother, father and two children, that became a support system for me. They invited me over for holidays like Christmas and Easter. They gave me the love and guidance I needed at that time. Just as with a regular family, there were occasional problems, but since my surrogate family was so much healthier and more positive than my own situation, it was much easier for me to be myself with them.

"Ironically, the family I chose as my surrogate eventually

became good friends with my actual mom and brothers and sisters. We've stayed in contact over the years, and when my husband and I were at the party at my parents', my 'adopted family' was also there."

Building a surrogate family need not be a rebellion or defiance toward your parents; it can be in their best interests. *The more your needs are met and the happier you are, the more you can learn to accept and love your parents without trying to change them.* Don't throw your surrogate support system in your parents' faces, make comparisons, or say, "Why can't you be like they are?" If your parents are jealous or upset that you spend more time with your surrogate family or support network, what they are most likely expressing is that they miss you. Rather than feeling angry or guilty, you can simply feel the love inherent in their desire to see you.

Your responsibility is to focus on what works. You can plan some holiday dinners and other "family-style" get-togethers with friends when it is difficult to feel relaxed and festive with your parents. Sometimes mixing friends and family at holiday occasions serves to diffuse the tensions and help you and your parents get along.

In some cases, you will need to extricate yourself from your family to provide the time and distance necessary to cut loose, grow and heal the relationship with the parents inside your head. If your "difficult" parent is alcoholic, abusive, emotionally disturbed or extremely controlling, the best way to make peace with him or her is first to extricate yourself and later to reestablish a healthier framework for relating to each other. When you set limits and demand your freedom from a martyr parent, he or she may try to make you feel guilty. In the same way, your dictator parent may become angry and try to intimidate you into relying on him or her again. What may seem initially like "breaking up" with your parents may be the key to an important *breakthrough* in your relationship. Letting go of old patterns, even if it means temporarily not seeing each other, is the first step in making the relationship work for both of you.

Instead of feeling guilty or afraid of your parents' reaction to your getting your needs met elsewhere, you should recognize that you must become more independent and self-reliant before you can make peace with them. As an adult, there is no crime in not needing anything from your parents! Even if your parents have created a "tender trap" in which they have maintained control over your finances, values and emotions in a way that has left you comfortable but dependent, you still may need to learn to be on your own.

Money is quite often a means of emotional blackmail. Some parents use money and financial strings to control or manipulate their children long after they have left the nest. In other cases, the promise of an inheritance when the parents die succeeds as a form of intimidation and control. The giving or withholding of money can be used to influence your choice of career, spouse, lifestyle or values, as well as controlling how often you visit, call or write your parents.

As an adult, you must recognize that you can no longer be emotionally blackmailed without your consent. Financial independence is a part of emotional independence. The purpose of building a surrogate family or support network is to help you discover that you *can* find emotional sustenance, belong to a group and have positive role models, love and affection without a lot of strings attached. Only then can you effectively deal with your parents in a healthy and genuine adult-adult relationship.

Guidelines for a Visit

Many clients who live in the same communities as their parents report feeling trapped, obligated or frustrated with routine visits. Instead of being enjoyable "want to" activities, visits home take on the burdensome quality of "have to" obligations. Many clients who live great distances from their parents feel trapped when they spend seven or fourteen days at a time under the same roof with their mother and father. It never fails to amaze me when I hear even successful, creative and independent adults describe their absolute obedience, guilt and lack of assertiveness when it comes to dealing with their parents effectively. Many a doctor, trial lawyer or corporate president remains controlled or intimidated by his or her parent!

In addition to making peace with the parents inside your head, a crucial step in improving your relationship with your mother and father is setting firm and effective guidelines for yourself to make each visit a success. In order to stop feeling burdened and start enjoying your get-togethers, you may have to recognize that *you and your parents might not be cut out to be roommates or best friends!* It doesn't work for you to give up all your power and let your parents dictate whom you will see, what you will do and how you will act when you visit their home. Nor should you assume that you are doing your parents a big favor with your visits. They may be as dissatisfied with the quality of the get-togethers as you are!

The cycle of missing each other, being disappointed with the visit, and then feeling resentful may be as painful to them as it is to you.

Based on the experiences of thousands of individuals, including myself, who have made peace with their parents, here are some guidelines you might consider for making your visits more successful:

—*Before you visit, do the exercises that will avert the conflicts you anticipate.* The techniques for working through resentments, anger, guilt and intimidation can eliminate much of your inner turmoil and potential conflict *before* they happen. Diligently using the exercises outlined in this book, you can safely assume that an ounce of prevention is worth ten pounds of cure!

—*Set a definite time limit on the duration of your visit.* Rather than spending your visit negotiating, defending or apologizing about how long you will stay, focus on quality instead of quantity. If a ninety-minute lunch is the most likely setting for a successful visit, don't feel guilty and spend six hours instead. If three days is the amount of time you and your parents tend to get along, don't insist that "love means having to stay under the same roof for two weeks."

—*Let your parents know in advance what other activities and people are on your schedule.* You don't have to spend every moment with your parents. They have lives of their own. You may have a variety of things you want to do in addition to seeing them. If the entire visit is spent on obligations and seeing relatives, neither you nor your parents will be in the best of moods to enjoy each other. If you want to see old friends, have private times with other people or simply have time alone or with your spouse or lover, you should let your parents know ahead of time so that your needs will be met without a struggle or hurt feelings.

—*Don't be afraid to set some ground rules.* If your parents can't help criticizing your home, its furnishings or your children, visit them at their home or at a neutral site. When you are going through emotional turmoil as a result of a divorce, job loss or illness and you are reluctant to listen to your parents' advice, don't feel guilty in delaying when you will see them or in limiting what topics you will discuss.

—*If you are traveling to visit your parents, stay with friends or at a nearby motel.* By giving yourself the time to relax after a long flight, the space to unwind and defuse your upsets, and the opportunity to do the anger ventilation exercises when needed, you will be far more likely to enjoy the time you actually spend with your parents. Also, you won't have to apologize for your, perhaps now very different, living habits, food preferences or needs for privacy.

—*Stay healthy and fit during your visit.* Instead of letting yourself fall back into old habits you may have had when you lived at home (and then resenting your parents for your weight gain or lethargy), remember to exercise, meditate, eat healthy and light meals, and relax whenever possible during your visit. At the same time, don't try to "reform" your parents. They are entitled to their own lifestyle and health habits, whether or not you approve!

—*Prepare your spouse or lover so you can support each*

other during the visit. If you visit your parents with a spouse or lover, be sure that person understands and is ready to deal with any emotional upsets you might be going through. Be sensitive as well to his or her needs, in case your partner feels neglected, excluded or uncomfortable at any time during the visit. Watch out for the approval trap! Your spouse or lover does not have to fall in love with your parents, nor do your parents have to adore and admire your partner. Without having to mediate or justify anyone's feelings, it's okay if things are simply cordial.

—*If you bring your children along, don't put the burden of the visit on them.* Sometimes you and your parents will avoid talking to each other and instead spend the entire time watching the children "perform." Not only can that be tiring for the children, but it can prevent you from working through your problems with your parents. In addition, some couples act as though three days with their parents—who have different eating habits, discipline styles and rewards than they—is going to spoil or damage the children. Instead of fearing that your parents are going to "ruin" your children, focus instead on the feelings, resentments and unresolved conflicts that are aroused in you by watching your parents play and interact with your children. You can learn a lot about yourself and your upbringing by watching closely, without having to "save" your children.

—*See the visits as an opportunity for growth, not as a painful burden.* Rather than avoiding or resisting conflicts, accept that from time to time problems will arise. Indeed, assume they will! As you continue to make peace with your parents, see each potential upset as an opportunity for being more effective in expressing anger constructively, setting effective limits and learning to express your love and acceptance. Favor the positive but don't be unrealistic in your expectations. By seeing the inner child within your parent and remembering to stop, relax and choose appropriate responses, you will be rewarded with more feelings of love and peace of mind.

5

Unraveling the Sexual Messages

Have you ever noticed how crowded your bedroom can get? You are there with your spouse or lover, but crowding around you are your fears, memories of past disappointments, resentments, pressures to perform, religious beliefs and social values as well as images you've picked up from movies and advertising. Taking up some very important space in the room are your parents and your partner's parents. Their conflicts, attitudes and rules are also influencing you. Though you may not be aware of it, you are receiving from all these sources sexual messages that may be interfering with your capacity to give and receive love.

As a character in one of Woody Allen's short stories once lamented, "I recalled not being able to perform with a sexy date . . . because some vague twist of her head reminded me of my Aunt Rifka." *

---

*Woody Allen, "Retribution," in *Side Effects* (New York: Random House, 1980).

Many people resist the suggestion that they learned about sexuality from their parents. They argue, "My parents didn't want to talk about it and I never saw them 'do it.'" Yet whether sex was openly discussed or hardly ever mentioned when you were a child, you learned a great deal from a variety of indirect and subtle clues. Your parents' marriage, good or bad, was your first exposure to an adult relationship and helped shape your attitudes about love, joy and sexuality. Many of the sexual messages that now affect your adult relationships were learned simply by observing your parents' interactions.

For example, if your parents argued a lot, you may have grown up thinking "love is a struggle." If they caused each other pain, you may have acquired the belief "you always hurt the one you love." If your father left your mother, died when you were young or failed to keep his promises, you may have decided "men can't be trusted." If your mother was unavailable or manipulative, you may have developed an overgeneralized attitude that "women are controlling." The sexual messages we learned from our parents were not always negative. For instance, if your mother and father were openly affectionate, appreciative of each other or comfortable with their sexuality, you are more likely to have grown up with a healthy attitude about love and sexual relationships.

Through verbal or nonverbal messages, your parents' sexual attitudes and fears were passed on to you and may still be influencing your feelings about touching, hugging, pleasure, love, commitment and marriage. For instance, if your mother or father was unavailable or unaffectionate to you, you may have internalized the message "I'm not lovable" or "I can never get what I want." If your father stopped kissing or hugging you when you reached puberty, you may have felt (as a female) "sex is dirty," or (as a male) "touching is for 'sissies.' " If your parents were traditionalists, you may have been pressured into conforming or rebelling against the stereotypes that "nice girls don't" or that "real men do."

Giving Yourself Permission

In order to begin to unravel your sexual messages, you need to examine how you were taught to hold yourself back sexually, to separate love from sex, or to deny and suppress your feelings of affection. For instance, can you enjoy your sexual feelings without suffering from guilt or performance anxiety? Can you be in love without feeling fearful or trapped? Can you ask for and receive sexual fulfillment without feeling selfish, undeserving or embarrassed?

Despite the "sexual revolution," most people still feel guilty experiencing high degrees of pleasure. They can perform like acrobats to please their partners, yet they may be left feeling empty regarding their own pleasure. They can succeed at work, sports and intellectual pursuits, yet they are blocked from fully expressing their love. They may be mature in most areas of their lives, yet remain frustrated in their sexual relationships.

If your parents taught you that pleasure is a highly regulated reward you must earn, you may have never learned that you deserve to be satisfied. Sexual pleasure may come very low on your list of important priorities in life. Relaxation and sensuality are often considered selfish or hedonistic and, based on the injunctions you were taught as a child, you may feel ashamed for wanting to enjoy yourself "when there's work to be done."

In most cases, your parents didn't simply express *their* feelings about pleasure and sexuality; the sexual messages were given added power by referring to absolute authority figures such as "the Bible forbids," "a 'good' person would never," "doctors say it is abnormal" or "don't let anyone know." Your parents or religious teachers may have taught you that pleasure is equated with sin or that virtue results from denying yourself, especially with regard to sex. Even if your parents didn't hold these values themselves, they may have wanted to "protect" you from being ostracized by a society that had more rigid values.

Rediscovering Your Sexuality

Sexual pleasure is neither a reward you must wait for nor an obligation you must endure. It is not a harmful obsession or an evil temptation. Love and sex are fundamental to your physical, psychological and spiritual well-being. The most profound spiritual teachers have argued that love is at the core of your being. Psychologists and physicians have known for years that sexual expression is a key to health, while sexual fears, anxieties and frustrations are a source of emotional and physical distress. Rather than being something you must avoid or limit, pleasure is an indication of health that includes joyfully being able to give more to others.

Sexual pleasure does not derive from how much, how many or how often, but from sharing love and becoming a more loving person. If sex has become a boring routine or if you and your partner have been taking each other for granted, by unraveling your sexual messages you will deepen your intimacy. If you have grown tired of short-term, arm's-length relationships, it may be time to work through the emotional barriers you acquired in childhood. If you feel as though you are always trying to please your partner and are unable to find your own satisfaction, reexamining your attitudes about sexuality and pleasure can help alleviate your problem.

The primary issue in unraveling your sexual messages is deciding whether you or your externally acquired attitudes will control your sexuality. Blindly accepting or blindly rebelling against parental values is not the answer. The secret of healthy adult sexuality is accepting your upbringing, evaluating it and affirming your own beliefs. Your psychological growth involves integrating the seemingly opposite values of *freedom and control.* Freedom comes as you release yourself from the sexual misinformation you learned from others, especially the inhibitions and pressures to perform. Control means choosing what works for you as an individual and learning when to say "No." Compulsively having to perform or to act out your fantasies becomes no freedom at all.

Making Your Own Rules

Do you have sexual values and preferences you can call your own? Or do you, like many people, rigidly follow or else rebel against the sexual attitudes that parents, peers and society have determined for you? Examining the ways you hold yourself back sexually or fail to ask for what you want from your spouse or lover will help you see who makes the rules in your life—you, your sexual messages or no one at all.

Lois' case is a good illustration of how we each must

discover for ourselves what we want from love and intimacy. A tall and slender thirty-eight-year-old woman, Lois met and married her husband Richard when she was twenty. She soon became pregnant and dropped out of college eighteen credits short of her degree. When she came to see me, she was the mother of two children, ages sixteen and twelve. She prided herself on being a "supermom," as well as a devoted wife. In addition, she had recently begun working part-time as a medical secretary to provide additional income for the family.

For several months, Lois had been suffering from anxiety attacks during which she would feel dizzy and weak, have a rapid pulse and sometimes hyperventilate. As the attacks worsened, she felt so anxious she stayed home from work. Unable to sleep, Lois feared that she was having a "nervous breakdown." Her husband insisted that the problem was the result of her working too hard, but Lois felt there was something else going on.

When she came to my office, she told me that the attacks had worsened following an incident that had occurred six weeks before. On her lunch hour, Lois had been browsing in a bookstore and met a good-looking, intelligent man who, after an enjoyable conversation, gave Lois his business card and suggested, "If you'd like to have lunch some day, please give me a call."

Lois kept their meeting secret, hid the phone number in her desk at the office and tried not to think about the handsome stranger, but a week later she impulsively called and asked him to join her at a nearby coffee shop for lunch. During the meal, the man said, "I find you very attractive and have been thinking about you ever since we met. If you're free some afternoon . . ."

Lois didn't reply, but she began having fantasies about him. A week later when she was running errands she stopped at a phone and dialed his number. Thrilled to hear from her, the man gave Lois directions to his apartment. After two drinks and the beginnings of a back massage, Lois was feeling very aroused but found she couldn't go through with the affair. Apologizing profusely, she hurried out of the apartment and was home just in time to meet her children returning from school.

The next evening, Richard's mother came to dinner. Cleaning up after the meal, Lois was alone in the kitchen when her chest seemed to tighten and she could hardly take a breath. She felt faint and had to be helped upstairs to lie in bed before her breathing returned to normal.

When I asked Lois to tell me what she was feeling about her life before the "almost affair," tears came to her eyes. She said she loved her husband and children, yet was unhappy with her marriage and particularly frustrated that she wasn't a better lover for her husband. According to Lois, "Richard's very physical and passionate, but I don't seem to want to have much sex any more. Most of the time I can't reach orgasm. For the last few years, it's felt like a burden and a chore." She felt guilty for even thinking about an affair and wanted to find some way to improve her sex life with her husband.

Lois also described the pressure she felt that she wasn't being a "good enough" wife and mother. "I have to work because we need the money. But Richard keeps telling me I should be home with the kids after school. His mother accuses me of neglecting my responsibilities. My mother thinks I should be at home and can't understand why I need to work. Between the three of them, I've got a nonstop chorus of advisers telling me how to run my life. I just can't keep it together any more."

As a homework assignment, I asked Lois to write a list of the sexual messages that were controlling her—not just about sexuality in the narrow sense, but also about sexual roles, family, love, marriage, pleasure and sensual enjoyment. Over the next week, she wrote a long list of "should's," "ought's" and "have to's," which included

—"I should always look nice and be cheerful."

—"The home is my responsibility. I'm to make sure the kids finish their homework, are clean, well-fed and well-behaved . . . Richard just needs to take out the garbage."

—"I should talk to Richard's mother every day but be careful not to make waves with her."

—"I should be more responsive in bed and want sex more often. I was taught that when you are in love, sex should be terrific."

—"I was warned by my mother not to let a good man slip by, to have children as soon as I got married and to do whatever it takes to keep my family intact."

The "I'll Be Happy When" Syndrome

After making her list, Lois began to understand why, in spite of seventeen years of following her parents' and now her mother-in-law's recipes for a happy marriage, she still wasn't happy. Nearly every one of her sexual messages promised that if she denied herself in order to please her husband, he in turn would please her and she would be happy.

As I explained to Lois, "In most marriages and relationships there is an unspoken contract that 'I'll be responsible for your happiness and you'll be responsible for mine.' The net result is two unhappy people. In this contract, if you're unhappy it's not your responsibility but your partner's. Like a continuation of the child's dependence on his or her parents for approval and satisfaction, most couples are striving for the other partner's approval and expecting the other partner to somehow make them happy. Quite often that means denying yourself, hoping for sympathy and support; then, when you don't get these, becoming resentful.

Over the next few weeks Lois began to take an inventory of all the times she denied herself by saying "No," "Wait," "Not now," "You're not good enough," "There's work to be done," "What will they think of me?" or "Do I deserve this?" This was especially important with regard to Lois' problem of not enjoying sex. She began to notice how her body shut down, how her anxiety increased and how she lost interest emotionally whenever she was in bed with Richard. "All it takes is one thought that I'm not doing enough, that I'm taking too long or that he's not going to like the way I look or the way I smell. I can be very turned on and then in an instant my thoughts change and I feel tense and uncomfortable. By that time I'm praying Richard will just finish and leave me alone."

To help her see the futility of postponing her own pleasure until her husband magically found a way to satisfy her, I told Lois about a client of mine who for ten years had been hoping that her husband would stroke her more gently an inch lower than he usually did. In ten years, she never asked and she never got. The longer she waited for him to find the right spot with the right caress, the more she resented him for being an "incompetent lover." Finally, at my suggestion, she put her hand over his and showed him the right location, pressure, speed and variations. Fortunately for that couple it wasn't too late. In many cases so much resentment builds up that by the time they try to make a change, either one or both partners want to get out of the relationship.

Lois smiled and said, "That's me. I'm always wishing Richard would somehow find the right spot. I know I'll be happy when he does, but I'm too embarrassed to ask."

Like many of us, Lois suffered from the "I'll be happy when" syndrome. In addition to hoping in silent despair that "I'll be happy when Richard finds the right spot," Lois had acquired a series of sexual messages that told her to postpone pleasure, keep her needs secret and wait until things miraculously got better. She was brought up to believe "I'll be happy when . . . I find the right man, I get married, I have children, we can afford a bigger house, the kids are away at school, the kids are grown, I find myself a job, Richard and I can afford to travel, Richard becomes a better lover, I become orgasmic." She was perpetually waiting for someone or something outside of her to make her happy. Even though she promised herself that happiness was right around the corner, there was always another "I'll be happy when" message just up ahead.

Communicating Your Needs and Desires

After she explored the ways in which she held herself back and was controlled by her sexual messages, Lois was ready to take the next step—to uncover and express her needs and desires. Personal growth includes insight *and* behavior change; insight alone is never enough. In order to unravel the sexual messages, you need to not only understand them but take steps to unfold your own sexual preferences and values.

Noticing how you hold yourself back to wait for others to satisfy you is an important first step. The next step is discovering how to enjoy your sexuality, communicate your needs and be responsible for lovingly getting your desires met.

As I explained to Lois, "You, not your partner or anyone you might meet, are primarily responsible for unfolding your sexuality, even if that means having to explain gently and in great detail what you enjoy most. Rather than feeling dependent or controlled by others, you need to make a commitment to your own satisfaction. You are bigger than the sexual messages and fears that you have internalized. You can choose to think, feel and behave differently from the way you were taught."

In order to overcome her sexual problem, Lois would have to explore her needs and desires on her own and then learn to assist Richard in understanding them. For her next homework assignment, I encouraged Lois to find an hour a week when the children and Richard weren't home. I told her to unplug the phones, slowly undress and spend at least thirty minutes in a luxurious bubble bath relaxing and exploring how to pleasure herself.

I warned her, "Many old prohibitions might run through your mind as you are in the bathtub. You may notice yourself having thoughts like 'You can't be doing this . . . it's dirty,' 'Shouldn't you be cleaning up the kitchen?' 'Richard is going to be furious,' 'What if his mother finds out?' and 'You're not supposed to enjoy yourself without a man.' When you have thoughts like these, let them merely pass through your mind without resistance and deliberately return to your pleasurable feelings."

Since Lois was afraid that if she enjoyed pleasuring herself on her own it would be harmful to her marriage, I assured her that "spending an hour or two a week exploring what turns you on is not going to make you self-indulgent. The parental message that pleasure is harmful confuses enjoying pleasure with excess in the pursuit of it. Eating an occasional scoop of ice cream is pleasurable; gorging yourself is harmful. The key is moderation. Denying yourself pleasure just makes it harder to enjoy those you love, including your husband and children. You are not going to 'use up' your sexual energy. On the contrary, the more you take time to enjoy and nurture yourself, the more you can give to others."

After Lois did her homework assignment a number of times, she discovered how erotic she could feel simply by touching and massaging various parts of her body. She said, "I get very aroused from rubbing not just my clitoris, but all over. My feet, thighs, breasts, neck, ears and face are all very sensitive. They each have a different and wonderful feeling when I stroke them vigorously, gently or with tickles."

On a weekend when Richard was at home and the children were away with friends, Lois took the initiative to share her newly discovered sexual feelings with her husband. She had been afraid that Richard would disapprove of or feel threatened by her self-explorations in the bathtub, but she found instead that he was relieved to see how much she could enjoy herself with him. He enjoyed following her advice and suggestions about how she liked to be touched. Over a number of weeks, Richard learned to be more gentle and slow in their lovemaking. According to Lois, "I had thought Richard and I were doomed to a boring sex life . . . now it's quite the opposite, very passionate, new and exciting."

In addition to improving her marriage, Lois' newfound ability to stop, relax and choose satisfaction whenever she felt tense or was about to be controlled by old messages also increased her enjoyment in other areas of her life. As she became more expressive of her needs around the house, she got more cooperation from Richard and the children. She enrolled part-time to complete the remaining credits for her college degree. She cut the number of phone calls and obligations to her mother-in-law.

Instead of postponing her own needs and pleasure for fear of offending others, Lois learned to be firm but gentle in asserting herself and making her life more enjoyable. The anxiety symptoms gradually diminished and eventually disappeared. While she reports that she still has occasional fantasies about other men, Lois describes how "the need is gone and so is the guilt. I can feel as sexy as I want whenever I want and yet I know that it's not going to get acted out in a way that would be inappropriate. I can keep my fantasies to myself or I can act them out with my husband."

Repeating the Past

By unraveling her sexual messages, Lois was able to stop repeating her pattern of self-denial and looking outside of herself for satisfaction. Until she realized that she could relate to her husband in a more creative and responsible way than she had been trained by her upbringing, she had felt trapped and powerless. In many cases, the psychological boundaries our parents placed on us as children become the self-restraints that hold us back as adults.

Your childhood relationship with your parents conditioned you to expect similar feelings in your adult intimate relationships. If you felt controlled or bullied by one or both of your parents, you may half-expect your partner to do the same. If you felt rejected as a child, you may be subconsciously creating the same pattern over and over again. If you tended to play the role of victim or rescuer in your family, you will likely play the victim or rescuer in your marriage or intimate relationships. If you felt trapped when you lived with your parents, you may feel the same desire to fight or flee when contemplating a committed relationship.

As a result of your upbringing, you may tend to overreact to anything in your adult relationships that bears even a vague resemblance to your past upsets. While you may accuse your partner of trapping or betraying you, in fact you may be trapped or betrayed by your unresolved emotions from childhood.

"She's Just Like My Mother"

Robert's case illustrates how to overcome the subconscious urge to expect from your spouse what you got from your parents. A successful business executive, Robert had made a habit of drinking regularly with his clients and corporate buddies. One night when Robert came home at two in the morning, he became enraged, seemingly over his wife Monica's "nagging" about his drinking. He said he was tired of her telling him what to do and warned her to "mind her own business."

Visibly shaken by this latest in a series of angry fights with her husband, Monica explained to me the next day that "Robert has two distinct aspects to his personality. He's an incredibly nice guy ninety percent of the time—fun, intelligent, sexy and very good with our son. But when he gets some alcohol in him and something triggers his anger, he's frightening. Lately I'm afraid he's going to destroy our marriage with his drinking. I don't know how to help him."

Even though Robert's drinking problem had begun to affect his marriage and work, he was reluctant to talk about it or come in for therapy. He told Monica, "There's nothing wrong with me. You're just overreacting." Only Monica's pleading resulted in Robert's finally agreeing to make an appointment.

An only child, he came from well-educated and affluent parents who "did everything for me. Whatever I wanted, they gave." Robert also knew from experience that every gift had a string attached. His parents helped him pay for the house he purchased during his first marriage, yet instead of putting the ownership in his name, they kept partial control of the property. According to Robert, they had reasoned, "This way your wife won't get her hands on it. It'll be safer in the long run." They also gave him a sizable trust account, but it too was in their name. While Robert had to pay taxes on the interest, he couldn't use the money without his parents' consent.

Throughout his life, Robert had felt controlled and then "rescued" by his parents. When he wrecked three cars during high school, they were there to save him. When his first marriage was breaking up, his mother was only too glad to first chastise him and then bail him out of his latest difficulty. Reflecting on his love/hate ambivalence for his parents, Robert commented, "I love the attention but I wish they would stop treating me like an irresponsible child."

Just as his parents had frequently criticized his first wife and suggested he get a divorce, so were they now undermining his second marriage. Each year, his mother sent Robert and his son expensive birthday presents, but never sent any to Monica. When Robert made the mistake of mentioning that he and Monica were arguing a lot, his parents were quick to suggest he get a divorce. No matter what Monica did as a housewife and mother, Robert's parents maintained the attitude that "our son deserves better."

When I asked Robert how he really felt about Monica, he said he wasn't sure. "I love her, but she's just like my mother. All she does is boss me around and watch every step I take. If I want to go out drinking with my buddies, that's my business. If I need a little fun on the side, she's just going to have to accept that's the way I am."

Robert's "fun on the side" had recently begun to include occasional affairs that were hurting Monica and threatening to destroy their relationship. In separate sessions with Monica, she described her reaction to the affairs. "I try not to be paranoid or ask too many questions, but it's funny . . . Robert is so sure I'm going to smother him like his mother does, he hears what he wants to hear. All I have to say is 'Will you be home for dinner?' and he flies into a rage that I'm a 'controlling bitch' just like his mother."

Breaking the Pattern

To help Robert see how close he was to wrecking his second marriage, I asked him to visualize two different scenarios of where he might be in ten years. In the first image, Robert would be the guy at the end of the bar, half drunk and complaining about how his first wife did this, his second wife did that, his third wife did something else and all women are blankety-blanks. In the second scenario, Robert would have quit his drinking, learned to communicate his anger effectively and rebuilt his marriage. Instead of being a self-destructive victim, he would be enjoying his wife and son.

Robert knew he couldn't afford a second divorce. "I love my son, and even with our troubles, I have this sense that Monica is the right woman for me. She loves me in spite of it all, and I feel awful when I hurt her." He admitted that he didn't know how to control his rage or say no to his desire for affairs. He also confided that, despite his boasts, "single life wasn't all it's cracked up to be."

When I asked Robert to make a list of the sexual messages he had acquired about love, marriage, sex roles and intimacy, his list included

"Women . . . you can't live with them, you can't live without them."

"When they marry you, they control you."

"A foxy lady doesn't wear apron strings."

"My mother always said that no other woman is good enough for her son."

"If a woman loves me, she'll put up with all my crap."

"When a woman is upset, you have to do whatever she says."

"You can't have fun and be married at the same time."

"I can't be trusted. I'm a spoiled child and need someone to keep me out of trouble."

As we discussed Robert's list, he began to see that most of his fears of intimacy and desire to have affairs were directly related to his resentments toward his mother. He described how whenever his parents were in town or called to give him advice, he felt even more trapped and angry with Monica. "No matter how well Monica and I are getting along, after I talk to my parents we invariably have a fight.

Talking with my folks gets me upset and so I drink. After that, anything triggers my anger."

To help Robert take charge of his life, I gave him the following recommendation, which is essential for clients with extremely controlling parents. "Sometimes when you are making major changes in your life, you may need to keep your parents at bay. If they say they want to visit, tell them this isn't a good time. If they start to overwhelm you with advice or criticism, tell them you appreciate their concern but you'll talk to them more about it some other time. Your health, well-being and marriage must take precedence over your parents' need to control you. Straighten out your life first—then you'll be in a much better position to deal more successfully with your parents."

Even though Robert admitted it was going to be difficult to stand up to his parents and change his own behavior, he knew it was time to break the patterns that were threatening to destroy his marriage. The first step in his treatment was to help him break his drinking habit. Along with taking Antabuse, a prescribed medication that helps overcome the urge to drink, Robert joined Alcoholics Anonymous to provide a support network for the changes he was undertaking. Next, he worked through a host of resentments toward his parents, his first wife and Monica. Robert noticed when he compared the lists that many of the resentments he had for Monica were very similar to resentments he had never resolved toward his mother.

Instead of letting his daily tensions build up or taking them out on Monica, he began to ventilate his angry feelings by pounding a mattress, screaming into a pillow or working out at the gym. To improve his overall health and peace of mind, he also began meditating twice a day, running at a local track each morning and improving his diet. Even though his parents tried to interrupt his progress more than once by offering him conflicting advice or questioning his ability to carry out these changes, Robert was gentle but firm as he told them, "You don't have to worry. I appreciate your concern and I'm doing fine."

The Vicious Cycle of Jealousy

A serious problem that remained for Robert and Monica was how to break the cycle of arguments, distrust and defiance that was eroding their marriage. Robert was still insisting that he had the right to have an "occasional" extramarital affair. Monica was still insisting that the affairs were selfish, hurtful and immature. Robert began making up clever excuses or being evasive regarding his whereabouts. Monica began to withdraw sexually as her resentments and distrust grew. As Monica withdrew, Robert's anger and desire for affairs increased. The more he stayed out late, the more she interrogated him. When Robert threatened to resume his drinking, Monica threatened divorce.

The problem for Robert was essentially one of either choosing his own rules and values or waiting for others to regulate his sexual behavior. Replacing one set of controls (his mother's) with another set (his wife's), Robert had never taken charge of his own sexuality. Instead of choosing responsibly, he was reacting with anger, defiance and an inability to say "No."

As I explained to Robert, "You think the issue is Monica —will she catch you or will she give you permission. That's no different from how you related to your mother. One of the ways you got your mother's love was by incurring her disapproval. When you were a 'bad boy' you got more of her attention. You're repeating the same pattern with Monica, as if saying, 'Show me you care by your jealousy.'

"Until you set limits for yourself and look at the consequences of your affairs, you will continue to feel trapped and controlled. Instead of waiting for Monica to be your disapproving parent, your job is to look at the mistrust and arguments you generate by your defiance. If you can recognize what the affairs are doing to your peace of mind, then *you* (not Monica, not your mother and not some other set of external messages) must make the marriage your priority and say 'No' when the urge arises."

For Monica, the problem was the same one faced by anyone whose partner is having an affair. She could have an affair to "get back" at Robert. She could suppress her feelings until her resentments piled up and she had to file for divorce. Or she could stop being a victim and learn to express her feelings and needs in a way that Robert could understand.

I pointed out to Robert and Monica that *what you focus your attention on in life grows stronger.* When their attention was consumed by the affairs, their relationship became dominated by mistrust, jealousy and defiance. Pretty soon they couldn't even look at each other without feeling angry. For Robert, this ensured that there could be no marital happiness and that only fleeting joy could be experienced by sneaking in an affair and getting away with it. For Monica, her energy was caught up in feeling neglected and monitoring Robert's behavior. Resentment and suspicion left them no room to enjoy their marriage. I explained to Robert and Monica that in addition to acknowledging the hurt feelings from the past, they could each gain a great deal by making their marital happiness, not the affairs, their focus. I suggested to Monica that rather than interrogating Robert or telling him that he's a bad person for what he's doing, she explain to him that she felt insecure, angry or lonely. "Instead of telling Robert what to do and getting nowhere, tell him how much you love him and miss the closeness, trust and physical affection the affairs have taken away. When you notice how much you miss the fun you used to have together, suggest specific ways the two of you can recapture the joy in your relationship."

In addition to following those suggestions, Robert and Monica began to rebuild their marriage by improving the communication and restoring the trust between them. Robert learned that he could feel attracted to other women but did not need to act upon his fantasies. With his anger resolved, he learned to take pride in being a good husband and father. He also began to admit when he felt trapped, controlled or smothered by their relationship. Working together to suggest solutions, Robert and Monica uncovered a variety of ways to improve their marriage so that they were close *and* had separate lives in proportion to both their needs.

Where There's Love There's Hate

Many couples assume that love means never having to say you're angry, sorry, irritated, turned off, hurt or upset. The illusion of the "perfect couple" is that problems won't arise, arguments are quickly forgiven and forgotten, and differences are for other people in less "perfect" relationships.

Just as you may have been told as a child that getting angry at your parents means you don't love them, so do many people conclude that anger and upsets have no place in a loving relationship. As soon as they find themselves irritated or upset, they assume "the thrill is gone" or "the honeymoon is over." It's important to understand that *all* intimate relationships have some ambivalence—where there is intense love there may occasionally be intense hate. Every relationship has its moments of stress and dissatisfaction. In fact, as part of having a healthy intimate relationship, you and your partner must assume that highly charged emotional conflicts will arise.

Unable to work through the painful and confusing feelings of love mixed with hate, most relationships remain in periodic turmoil or chronic despair—these days, that means breaking up and starting the pattern all over again with another partner. Single and divorced people find themselves settling for "arm's-length" relationships that break up as soon as the resemblances to past upsets and suppressed hurts arise. The fear of getting trapped again—of re-creating the personal hell of childhood—is overwhelming. Married couples find themselves more alienated and dissatisfied the longer they let the emotional remnants of past parental conflicts control their relationship. Many find their passion blocked and sex a boring routine once ambivalence takes over.

"At First It Was Like a Dream Come True"

The case of Fran and Perry illustrates the difficulties of working through the love/hate feelings that arise in any long-term relationship. When they first met on a late-night coast-to-coast airplane flight, Fran and Perry found themselves in a storybook infatuation. A strikingly attractive sales representative for a cosmetics firm in Los Angeles, Fran was thirty-four when she "fell in love at first sight" with Perry, forty-two, a ruggedly handsome architect from Washington, D.C. Within a few weeks they were commuting between her apartment near the Pacific Ocean and his townhouse overlooking the Potomac River at least three times a month for what both described as "the best sex I'd ever imagined." Most of the time when they reunited after ten or twenty days apart, Fran and Perry would make love on the floor of his apartment because "we couldn't wait until we got into the bedroom." Sometimes on long weekend drives in the country, they would pull off to the side of the road and make love "in the car, on a blanket . . . wherever and whenever."

Perry remembers thinking to himself at that time, "She's the exact opposite of my mother. My parents were so uptight sexually, I used to believe they only 'did it' three times—just enough to conceive my two brothers and me. One time when I was ten or eleven, I walked into my mother's bedroom while she was zipping up her dress. She screamed and pulled away. I couldn't help but feel like a criminal."

In contrast, "When Fran and I first met it was like a dream come true. Not just the way we made love, which was incredible, but how close we felt to each other. I believed she could read my mind—she knew exactly what I wanted and she always said the right thing. I'd never been so in love."

Fran also described her excitement at finding someone who was "not at all like my father." After being raised by a strict disciplinarian father, Fran had repeatedly attracted men "who were very dominating and cold." While her father had never resorted to physical violence, he had often intimidated Fran and her younger sister with his angry stares, cruel statements and the belittling ways he kept them in line.

Fran recalled that when she was twelve years old, she was strongly attracted to her exceptionally handsome father. "In those days he was a bully most of the time, but with me he could be very playful and affectionate. Then all of a sudden my body started to change and he became icy and withdrawn. He even refused to hug me or kiss me goodnight anymore. One time when he was mad at me about my grades in school, he accused me of trying to seduce one of his business partners. I had on a pair of shorts not so different from what everyone was wearing in those days. First he called me a 'prick tease' and then told me that if I didn't stop acting like a slut, he was going to send me away to a boarding school. That night I locked the door to my bedroom and cried my eyes out. Even my mom took his side, saying that I'd done something to turn his business partner on. I knew I hadn't, but no one would believe me."

The incident Fran described is unfortunately not an uncommon experience for a woman when she reaches puberty. The father may feel guilty for his sexual attraction to his daughter. By withdrawing and/or blaming her for his feelings, he leaves the impression that his daughter is "naughty" or is being rejected because of something she did wrong. In some cases, when the daughter uses her emerging seductiveness to win back her father's attention, further conflicts arise. Both father and daughter, or in the reverse case mother and son, must learn that these sexual feelings are natural and delightful, as long as they are not acted out in a way that is inappropriate. Since father and daughter will not have sex together, they can enjoy their mutual admiration and attraction in a nonthreatening way.

When Fran met Perry, she felt relieved that "I'd finally found a man who was honest and relaxed about his sexuality.

Perry wasn't pushy or demanding like most men. He knew how to be warm, affectionate, sincere and tender. In those early days, we used to stay up all night talking about our dreams and plans. I felt like I was seventeen all over again. It was wonderful, and after six months of long-distance phone calls and tearful goodbye scenes at airports, I was ready to start living together and maybe get married."

"All I Could Think About Was Getting Out"

The minute Fran announced her wish to share an apartment, the problems began. Perry said he wasn't ready to stop dating other women. Even though Fran let him know how much it hurt her to think of him with other women, he insisted that, for a while at least, he needed to "hold on to his options." According to Perry, "I'd been burnt once before in my first marriage and I wasn't going to make the same mistake of rushing things again. Fran used to say that she loved me for being so independent and carefree. Then all of a sudden she resented me for not wanting to be committed and tied down."

Fran described how she felt "used and taken for granted by Perry. I was his sexual toy, weekends only, for his total pleasure without any commitments. We started arguing about whether I should move to D.C. or he should come to L.A. The more we argued, the more I saw how selfish and stubborn he was.

"I began to put up my defenses sexually and that made him start to get demanding. All he had to do was touch my hand and I could feel the pressure on me that he wanted intercourse. So I'd tell him no and he'd say I was being a 'cold bitch'—that all he wanted was to be close to me. I didn't believe a word he said at that point. Even though he kept insisting that he still loved me, all I could think about was getting out."

When Fran began to withdraw sexually, Perry felt rejected and angry. Sometimes he tried to coax Fran into having sex; at other times he would silently resent her. The more she said no, the more Perry's rage began to block his tenderness. Their mutual distrust became self-fulfilling: the more he demanded affection, the more she withdrew; the more she withdrew, the more resentful and demanding he became.

Anticipating rejection, Perry began to turn his resentments into sarcastic comments. One night when Fran put on her favorite low-cut dress for an important formal dinner with Perry's business associates, Perry accused her of being a "tease." Grabbing her suitcase and catching the next plane to Los Angeles, Fran later said she felt "like a crazy woman. I felt like I wanted to kill him and hated the fact that I still loved him."

Can Love Last?

Fran and Perry both knew that if they continued to remind each other of their parents' worst qualities, they would eventually split up. Their strong and unresolved love/hate for each other would then be carried along as "emotional baggage" into their next relationships. Perry would find a way to feel sexually rejected and bitterly resentful with the next woman he loved. Fran would find a way to feel sexually dominated and taken for granted by the next man she loved. The pattern would continue to repeat itself unless and until they learned to deal with the inevitable challenge of unresolved sexual messages.

When Fran and Perry came in for therapy, I said, "You both realize that you're still in love. The question is whether you are motivated to break through your patterns now or go your separate ways." Fortunately, they came in early enough and both were still optimistic they could be lovers again. To help them regain the trust and romance they had enjoyed when they first met, I offered the following exercises and aids, which can be used with a loved one to reduce sexual barriers and emotional blocks.

I. REKINDLING THE ROMANCE

Like most couples in conflict, Fran and Perry would become tense, defensive and emotionally withdrawn whenever they were together. They had trouble making eye contact. When they were arguing, neither was listening. Each felt unappreciated by the other partner. Both were suffering from trying to suppress and deny their feelings of love.

To help remind them of why they were together at all, I asked them to sit face to face, making eye contact as they exchanged acknowledgments with each other. This simple exercise has very few rules: the person whose turn it is to speak describes in one or two specific sentences what he or she appreciates about the person listening; the person listening must take in the acknowledgments, say either "Thank you" or "I got it" after each one, and repeat the communication as close to the original as possible without adding anything; denying, arguing or saying "Oh no, I'm not really as good as you say . . ." is prohibited.

Doing this exercise was a radical departure from Fran and Perry's usual mode of communication, which consisted of accusations, demands, threats and counterthreats. While at first the tension between them seemed to build, it quickly peaked and then slowly melted away. A few minutes after Perry began listing the things he appreciated about Fran, her eyes began filling with tears. Immediately thereafter, Perry's eyes were moist, too. Neither could deny the love that was underneath the struggle of wills in their relationship.

2. RESOLVING PAST HURTS

During the months of arguments and disagreements, Fran and Perry had hurt each other's feelings countless times. While both regretted that they had hurt each other, I suggested they accept the fact that part of a loving relationship is conflict and that "love means stuff is going to come up." Instead of resisting or denying the inevitable conflicts, they needed to learn to deal with each other's hurt feelings so that they could recover from their disputes and move on to more enjoyment.

In a face-to-face exercise similar to the one described above, I asked them to take responsibility for their own hurt feelings and describe gently and without blame or attack what each needed from the other to prevent future upsets. Once again the person speaking was not to be interrupted, while the person listening was only to say "Thank you" or "I got it" and then to repeat the communication.

Fran began sharing a few past hurts, with Perry repeating each one back to her as nonjudgmentally as possible:

> "It hurt me when you called me a 'tease.' I'd prefer if you told me how you feel about the way I dress without making any sexual remarks."

"It hurt me when you said you didn't want to marry me yet. I'd feel better if you were more open about your fears so that I wouldn't take the rejection as personally."

"It hurt me when you said my work was less important. I need your respect and wish you could see how much my work means to me."

Perry then shared the following hurts he had suffered, which Fran repeated back to him without judgment or defensiveness:

"It hurt me when you said our fights were all my fault. I need to know that we're working together on our relationship and that we're both willing to change."

"It hurt me when you said I'm only trying to have sex with you. I need you to see how much I love you and that I'm willing to stay together even when we're not having sex."

"It hurt me when you wouldn't return my calls. I need to be able to communicate with you even when we're having troubles."

Fran and Perry were able to work through a number of their past resentments and hurt feelings by stating their points of view briefly, in specific terms and with a *commitment toward a positive outcome.* Instead of blaming or accusing each other with self-righteous anger, they continued to make eye contact, speak in a warm and nonthreatening tone of voice, and focus on what could be done to satisfy both their needs in the relationship. For the first time, they both felt that their hurt feelings were being acknowledged and understood.

3. UNBLOCKING THE FLOW OF LOVE

Another exercise that was especially effective for Fran and Perry was to make a list of "the ways I've been blocking love in my life . . ." This technique helps you stop blaming your partner and start seeing how you contribute to the relationship's failure to work. Since both partners were acting defensive and hostile as soon as they reminded each other of their parents, they needed to unravel how they had fallen into those patterns and how they could break out of them. Admitting to yourself and your partner how *you* inhibit your pleasure, keep up your defenses and prevent feelings of trust and intimacy can help you free yourself.

On Perry's list, he included

"The way I've been blocking love in my life is . . ."

—By having lots of relationships instead of committing to one.

—By getting angry and demanding about sex.

—By working too hard at my job and then needing sex as a tension release instead of as a way to express love.

—By viewing women as conquests and trophies, not as people or friends.

—By trying so hard to make Fran have an orgasm that I stop feeling tender or listening to her feelings.

On Fran's list, she described

"The way I've been blocking love in my life is . . ."

—By insisting on a commitment instead of feeling how much Perry loves me.

—By blaming Perry for the problems in our relationship.

—By shutting off my feelings and withholding sex to punish him and gain power.

—By making Perry feel insecure and angry.

—By thinking I might die if I can't have Perry's love.

By admitting honestly how *you* stand in the way of receiving love, you no longer need to attack or blame your partner. The patterns you uncover may have been the reasons why previous relationships did not work, and will surely carry over into your next relationship if you don't work through them this time. When you recognize and change your patterns of blocking love, your life becomes more richly rewarding.

4. SHARING FUN IN AND OUT OF BED

In order to help Fran and Perry overcome their sexual conflicts and put more enjoyment and satisfaction into their relationship, I suggested the means that have helped many couples find a level of passion and romance far richer than the sexual thrill of their initial infatuation.

—*Lightening up.* Too often couples fall into the trap of working excessively on their relationships. The more they try to fix the relationship, the heavier their problems seem. All work and no play can make for a burdensome relationship. The goal of unraveling your sexual messages is different—it is to lighten up your intimate relationship so that you and your partner can relax together and have fun.

—*Nonsexual touching.* Instead of viewing every act of physical affection from Perry as a demand for intercourse, Fran learned to relax and regain her feelings of intimacy and trust by enjoying a number of weeks of nonsexual touching with Perry. As she described it, "I like to be tender and cuddly, not rushed or expected to perform. Perry and I spent night after night simply holding hands, lying next to each other, stroking faces, or just holding each other without doing anything sexual. Some nights we massaged each other's back, neck, feet, hands and face. Other nights we took a bath or a shower together. As a result, we were like teenagers again—long, passionate kisses and lots of caressing. It was even more exciting than when we first met because we were both so surprised by how much we still could turn each other on."

—*Nonorgasmic lovemaking.* As a next step in breaking free of the pressures of goal-oriented sex, Fran and Perry began experimenting with extended lovemaking sessions in which one or both partners consciously overcame the urge to reach orgasm. Sometimes this meant lengthy sessions of foreplay combined with long intermissions of relaxed breathing and gentle touching or massage. At other times they simply breathed, slowed down and relaxed at the peak of excitement without Perry's ejaculating or Fran's reaching an orgasm. At still other times they would vary speeds and intensity at will, often reaching levels of intimacy they had never imagined possible.

—*Adventure days.* Since Fran and Perry realized that they both came from parents whose relationships had been filled with "should's," "ought's" and "have to's" in which each partner took the other for granted, they decided to do everything they could to avoid getting locked into boring routines. As a result, they set up creative adventure days. At least once a month, either Fran or Perry would take turns being responsible for a day trip or weekend outing that proved to be a memorable adventure. One month Perry took Fran on all of her favorite rides at a nearby amusement park. Another weekend Fran took

Perry on an art tour to the museums and galleries he "never had time for." One weekend Perry encouraged Fran to spend the entire time lounging in bed while he cooked, cleaned and catered to her sexual fantasies.

—*Unbirthday gifts.* With little effort or planning, Fran and Perry began to give each other surprises: gifts, poems, flowers, love letters and songs when they least expected them. Instead of waiting for birthdays or holidays, they repeatedly surprised each other with special treats that never failed to make the other person feel appreciated and loved.

—*Three appreciations a day.* Several times a week before going to sleep, Fran and Perry did a simple exercise that has helped many couples stay together and avoid taking each other for granted. While the other person listened without interrupting, Fran or Perry would take turns sharing "Three things I appreciated about you today are . . ." Even if the three things were as mundane as "I liked it when you told the plumber to clean up his mess" or "I appreciated it when you emptied the dishwasher," their relationship benefited from their ability to acknowledge each other verbally for the day-to-day things that made it successful. Three appreciations a day keep the psychotherapist away!

While Fran and Perry are well aware that parental messages and past resentments may come up from time to time, they are prepared to deal with them without blaming or attacking each other. Within a year after they came in for counseling, they had reached a deeper level of commitment. Soon afterward they were married and they have continued to grow as individuals and as a couple.

6

Dealing with Parental Aging, Dying and Death

When any of us faces the aging, dying or death of a parent, we are confronted by feelings that often seem overwhelming. Your reluctance to talk about these matters may prevent you from adequately dealing with the realities of your parent's condition. The need to take care of your parent may bring up suppressed feelings about the ways in which he or she failed to be supportive of you. The difficult burden placed on your emotions, finances and family may be combined with the belief "I can't say no."

Quite often people feel guilty for having thoughts like "She was in so much pain I just wanted it to end," "I couldn't let him come live with us," "It's not fair that I always have to bear the burden" or "The things I couldn't stand have gotten worse with age." While these reactions are common and do not mean that you love your parent any less, many of us were taught that to have mixed emotions about our parents is selfish or ungrateful. As a result, we may pretend to be selfless and saintly in the presence of our aging or dying parent when in fact anger or fears are stirring inside. Some of us bend over backward to cater to the demands of an aging or dying parent in order to be forgiven for past indiscretions or to prove that unlike our formerly favored brother or sister, we are really the "good child" in the family. Others of us block out anything negative when recalling our dying or departed parent so that we can pretend our resentments never existed.

•Grace, fifty-four, is married and has three grown children. When describing her eighty-year-old mother, who has rheumatoid arthritis with chronic pain in most of the joints of her body, Grace says, "While my mother is never directly demanding, she is obviously suffering terribly. I feel helpless in the same way I would feel helpless when an infant is terribly sick and there is really nothing much I can do to help. The worst part is how guilty I feel when I find myself 'tallying up'—my mother took care of me only until I was seventeen and on my own. I've been 'on duty' for her the last twenty-six years."

•Dolores, twenty-five, is a divorced mother of two children whose fifty-eight-year-old father recently suffered a debilitating stroke that left him partially paralyzed and unable to speak. According to Dolores, "I spend every minute I can at the hospital, but I don't even know if he's aware of my presence. Mom is a wreck and she needs someone to be there. With two kids and a full-time job, it's taking a toll on me. I'm ashamed for thinking about myself, but if I don't, who else will?"

•When Karl, twenty-nine, flies back to Chicago once a year to see his father and stepmother, he always stops at the cemetery to visit his mother's grave. Even though she died in a car accident when he was eight years old, Karl describes how "the feelings are still confusing. I'm angry that she left without saying goodbye. Whenever something good happens for me, I'm sad she couldn't be there to share it. I wish I could get over my feelings, but even after all these years there's a sense of frustration that we barely got to know each other."

•Connie, thirty-eight, recently returned from a surprise birthday party for her father in which, she recalls, "there was a moment of shock when I looked at my parents and saw for the first time how much they've aged in the past two years. I never really thought about them growing old, yet all of a sudden it hit me that one day they would die. Seeing how they'd aged made me feel old, too. It scared me, and while I tried to think about the birthday party, I couldn't stop wondering whether they were as frightened about death as I was."

"Do We Have to Talk About It?"

Even though the problem of dealing with aging is something we all face sooner or later, our society still treats it as an unspoken taboo. By denying the inherent ambivalence we all have about death, and especially about the aging or dying of a parent, we force our anger, fears and regrets to come out in indirect and unfortunate ways. Sometimes holding in mixed feelings keeps you from loving your parent while he or she is alive. At other times it may cause you to make unintentionally hurtful comments or inadequate decisions when that parent really needs your support. If you fail to work through your mixed feelings for a parent who has become dependent or has died, you may undermine your health as well as your relationship with your spouse, children and siblings.

In most families, discussions about aging and death are avoided because of the awkward feelings aroused by the topic. When a parent needs to make a difficult decision, such as whether or not to have an operation, too often the children are unable or unwilling to participate. When a parent needs to talk about his or her will, estate or insurance policies, too often the children interrupt the conversation with comments like "Don't be so morbid" or "Do we have to talk about it?" When a parent needs to articulate the painful emotions associated with a terminal illness, too often the children prevent the parent from sharing feelings by saying, "Don't worry. You're going to be fine."

Whether covering up one's own fears or trying to protect the other person, the silence between children and parents is more often than not a barrier to the love and communication both need so desperately. In most cases, the parent learns to avoid bringing up painful subjects, to retreat into isolation and to give up the attempt to reestablish closeness. The children of the dying parent are left without having had the chance to express their love or to fully understand the process of a parent dying. Dealing with an aging parent can be seen as a guilt-ridden burden or an opportunity for intimacy. Whether or not you deal effectively with your mixed feelings is the key for breaking through long-held barriers and emotional distance.

This chapter will help you understand the often difficult challenges of dealing with parents who because of age, illness or their own personality needs become demanding of their children. It will help you sort through your own conflicting emotions about parental dying and death. By learning to make peace with your ambivalence, you can reach a new level of understanding and love for your mother and father, whether they are alive or not. Even more important, by learning to deal with the challenges you face, you will be able to regain your peace of mind and eliminate the feelings of guilt that often leave lasting emotional scars long after a parent has died.

The Reversal of Roles

Over a period of years, or suddenly as the result of a serious illness, your active, self-reliant parent may become dependent and physically limited. Poor concentration, memory loss, bodily complaints, difficulties with walking or driving, lack of social contacts and shrinking financial resources can make even the most independent aging parent look to his or her children for advice and support. Quite often your parent may become short-tempered, demanding, manipulative or withdrawn as a result of these significant physical and emotional changes.

Adult children of aging parents frequently comment that their parents are "self-preoccupied" or "closing down." Their parents' lives have become much narrower as a result of retirement, lack of mobility or physical illnesses. "Difficult" parents who were martyrs or dictators become even more so as a result of their increased dependence on you. Conflicts and resentments that may have been dormant for years suddenly reemerge as your relationship with your aging parent takes up more of your time and attention.

Even though you may be at the stage of life when your career, marriage, children or desire for independence are your highest priorities, the fact that your parent truly needs your assistance confronts you with a serious dilemma—what are you willing and able to offer your parent to deal with his or her justifiable needs? Adults in this situation are often caught between the demands of their teenage or young adult children and those of their aging parents; like a "lost generation," they feel pressured emotionally and financially from both sides.

Whether you were the "favorite" or the "black sheep," whether you have the time, energy, funds or desire to help, and whether you feel competent to deal with the challenges your parent faces, the problems nonetheless fall into your lap. Instead of being the child who looks to your parent for help and guidance, you are now expected to answer questions like "I have a pain in my side . . . do you think it's serious?" "Should I sell the house and move into a retirement home?" "Should I get rid of the housekeeper?" "Should I take the medication even though I'm feeling better?" "Should I stay with you until I find another place?" and "Should I buy a new television set or do you think this one can be fixed?"

As much as you might resent your new role or feel inadequate to give your parent what he or she needs, the challenge of dealing effectively with an aging parent can be an opportunity for tremendous growth and increased love. Being forced to address the needs of your parent may be the first time you have seen him or her as a person and not just as a parent. Breaking out of the parent-child role that has marked your relationship from the start, you may discover new ways of meaningfully being together.

"We Never Planned It This Way"

Paula's case demonstrates some of the problems and joys of dealing with an aging parent. A forty-year-old woman with a husband and two sons, ages nineteen and seventeen, Paula came from a family of five children. According to Paula, "My two sisters are both divorced; one of my brothers lives in Oregon and the other one never got married. So when Mom died unexpectedly and Dad needed a place to stay until he found a place of his own, we consented to fix up the extra room in our house. It was the obvious solution because I was the only one of the children who was 'settled down.' Even though Dad and I weren't all that close when I was growing up, we knew he couldn't rely on the others. But we also thought it was temporary—with my eldest son away at college and his brother graduating soon from high school, I was looking forward to my hard-earned freedom."

For the first six months, the living arrangement wasn't a problem. Paula found him to be "a little helpless, like a 'lost soul' without Mom. For years Mom had worried that Dad would die of a heart attack. She pampered him tremendously and fretted over his diet and exercise. None of us ever expected Mom to go first."

Even though Paula's father was somewhat withdrawn and began drinking more than he had when his wife was alive, there were no major arguments between Paula and her father. Paula related how "he was trying hard not to be a burden, and he was such a good influence on our son during a difficult senior year of high school. He helped out in the kitchen sometimes and kept his room neat and clean. Even so, my husband and I repeatedly asked ourselves, 'When is he going to move out?' We never planned it this way and it was as though our lives had been put 'on hold' while we waited for Dad to make up his mind."

After her father had been living with them for almost a year, there were increasing signs of trouble. According to Paula, "I began to notice that I was becoming an emotional wreck. Dad's drinking was getting on my nerves. I was forever trying to make sure my father and my husband didn't argue or get in each other's way. Dad was increasingly absent-minded and would misplace his keys, his wallet and his eyeglasses. One time when he was looking for his favorite belt, I accidentally blew up and said something mean I later regretted. My husband and I hadn't taken a vacation in almost eighteen months and our sex life had dwindled to practically nothing. Even though my father wasn't to blame, I felt like I was living in his house, abiding by his rules."

One day when Paula's sons were home on vacation from college, Paula's father became irritated by their loud music and headed downstairs to the basement to tell them to turn it down. However, he slipped on the stairway, fell and broke his wrist. According to Paula, "We all felt terrible. The kids felt guilty and blamed themselves. My husband said we were fortunate he hadn't suffered a more serious accident. From then on we were walking on eggshells trying not to do anything that might upset Dad."

When Paula came in to see me to discuss her problems, one of the first questions I asked her was "Does your father know what he needs to do next about finding a place of his own?" Her immediate reponse was "I don't know. We've never asked him." Like many people who are forced to take care of an aging parent, Paula felt caught in the middle. As she described it, "On the one hand I feel guilty whenever I see how lonely he is; at the same time I can't imagine how to stand up and say to him, 'Dad, it's time you moved out.' "

After Paula worked through a number of resentments toward her father and began to discover some of the ways that she held herself back whenever he was around, I recommended that she convene a family meeting to address the unspoken issues that were causing conflicts in her family. At first Paula thought I meant that she, her husband and her father should meet. Instead, I encouraged her also to involve her brothers and sisters. As I explained, "Just because you agreed to let your father stay at your home for a temporary period does not mean you must be saddled with all the responsibilities thereafter. This is a family problem that includes all family members."

The first obstacle Paula had to overcome was the resistance of her brothers and sisters. Trying to find a date and time when each could attend was initially "next to impossible." While one of Paula's younger sisters was agreeable, the other three siblings used arguments like "Stop worrying about Dad . . . he'll be all right if you give him time" or "I'd like to help, but things are very busy right now." Finally, with her sister's help, Paula was able to arrange a time when the entire family, including her father, could attend.

Paula and her husband needed to sort through their mixed feelings. In many families with this kind of problem, decisions are made without consulting spouses. While the solutions might be what the children of the parent in question desire, spouses often feel ignored or inconvenienced. After giving the matter a great deal of thought and discussion, Paula and her husband concluded that their feelings were similar—they both knew that they didn't want to let the present situation continue but they didn't have the heart to just tell her father to leave.

Even worse than the failure to consult spouses, many families make decisions that affect an aging parent without consulting him or her. In Paula's case, she began the first family meeting by asking her father to describe his needs and wants in his own words. According to Paula, "I thought Dad was going to talk about how he felt uncomfortable living with us, but instead all he did was deny that there was a problem. Throughout the first meeting, Dad was withdrawn and evasive. He had too much pride to ask for help or to admit how lonely and unhappy he was. He said things like 'I'm not helpless, you know' and 'Everything's fine . . . you're all making a big deal about nothing.'

"My brothers and sisters also used the meeting to score points with Dad. They agreed with everything he said and offered to have him over for dinner, take him on vacations and call more often—all the things they had never done in the past eighteen months and would probably never do unless confronted.

"That night I didn't sleep a wink and wound up crying alone in the den. You told me, Dr. Bloomfield, that the first meeting is often just a start and doesn't yet solve the family issues, but I never thought it would be so dishonest and frustrating. At four in the morning Dad came down and asked why I was crying. I told him the truth—that I loved him and I didn't know how to tell him that I needed my own place again. Admitting that I needed to be independent was even tougher that night than when I first moved out at age eighteen.

"To my surprise, Dad's face lit up and he laughed. 'Paula, you and I are a couple of real jerks,' he said. Then he admitted what I'd suspected all along. It was getting uncomfortable for him as well living under the same roof. For almost two years, we'd been lying to each other trying to cover up what we both needed for fear of hurting each other. Once we got that out of the way, we talked the rest of the night about everything: Mom, his parents, what he was like as a teenager, what he enjoyed about his friends and what he couldn't stand about them. It was the first time in a long while he and I had talked like old friends instead of like father and daughter.

"He spoke about his fears of being alone and his anger at Mom for dying. In the past, I would have immediately tried to talk him out of those feelings and said, 'Oh, Dad, you don't mean what you're saying.' This time I just sat there and held his hand while he cried a little. I told him how conflicted I felt in my wanting to be there for him as well as my husband and children. He offered that one of the hardest parts of old age was the fear of 'becoming a burden on your children.'

"When we got around to talking about moving, he admitted that besides the fear of being alone he had a serious dilemma. He wasn't sure he could afford the steep rents in the nicer areas. When I assured him that we would be glad to help, I saw his expression change and he seemed to breathe easier."

Another family meeting was held the following week to iron out the remaining details. After Paula's father described his financial problems, the family members began to suggest ways they could alleviate his worries. For the next six weeks, family members took turns helping Paula's father look for an affordable and attractive apartment. The one they found was bright and well-managed, only two miles from Paula's home. In addition, they arranged to have a housekeeper come in four days a week to clean and cook.

While the transition period was at times difficult, and Paula described "feeling very responsible and making sure I called Dad every day," after a few months her father began to have a far more active social life than he had had when he was living with Paula and her family. Through a local social service organization, Paula's father joined a senior citizens' club with weekly dances, a sightseeing program with frequent bus tours and a weekly film and discussion series at a local public library.

Having Realistic Expectations

While not every family crisis turns out as smoothly, Paula's case provides some guidelines for handling the conflicting feelings brought on by the needs of an aging parent. By dealing with her own emotions, Paula was better able to take charge of the situation. By discovering how she held herself back with her father, she became more honest in asserting her own and her family's needs and offering potential solutions. By involving her spouse and making sure his feelings were aired and considered, she avoided unnecessary problems that can be destructive to even the most stable marriage. By involving the other family members and repeatedly focusing on "What does Father want?" and "What can each of us provide without being unrealistic?" she helped the family resolve the issues no one had wanted to discuss. In the process she brought the family closer together and avoided further isolation of her siblings. Finally, by using the local social service and community groups, Paula was able to be of assistance to her father without becoming his full-time caretaker or surrogate parent.

The key to dealing effectively with the challenges of an aging parent is to have realistic expectations. You should take on those things you *can* do without beating yourself up for those things you cannot change about your parent or his or her condition. Every parent presents different challenges and reacts differently to the offer of help from his or her children. By first dealing with your own mixed feelings and then making a clear offer of what you can provide, you will be more likely to avoid unnecessary conflicts.

An important fact that many children of aging parents fail to recognize is that some physical and emotional symptoms of old age are highly treatable. Quite often your parent's bodily complaints, failing memory, confusion and insomnia can be diagnosed and treated after a complete medical examination. What appears to be organic brain damage or senility may be a symptom of depression, diabetes or hearing loss. A number of adult children complain that their parents don't seem to be listening to them because they are so absorbed in their problems. Some of this may be due to the fact that their parents are simply unable to hear what's being said. A competent evaluation of these and other symptoms by a physician who specializes in diseases of the aged is recommended.

Beyond the physical and emotional challenges of old age, there are still many opportunities available to you and your aging parent for building intimacy and trust. This may be the chance to find out more about your parent's childhood, listen to his or her memories of significant historical events, and hear the family stories about Aunt Betsy and Great-uncle Louis. You may want to use a tape recorder or videotape machine to record your family legacy for posterity. You may want to find out more about what your first few years of life were like. Now that you are an adult, the stories and insights can be extremely valuable and moving. Having your parent look through old photos and recall the surrounding events can be a rewarding experience for both of you.

Living with Uncertainty

For many people, the most difficult challenge of dealing with an aging parent comes during the months or years after your mother or father is found to have a terminal illness. You live in limbo, as no one knows for sure how long your parent will live. You want to do something, but feel helpless when there is nothing to be done. Not only are you dealing with your own inner turmoil but you are expected to deal with your parent's needs as well.

When we are confronted with the reality of our mother or father facing imminent death, no matter what our level of education or expertise, most of us still feel awkward, frightened or overwhelmed. To illustrate some of the struggles and triumphs that can occur when a parent is dying, a client of mine described what she went through during the months her father was dying of lung cancer.

A thirty-two-year-old assistant producer for a television talk show, Margaret remembers:

"When I went home for Christmas last December, I knew something was wrong the minute Dad came to greet me in the driveway. Usually a powerfully built and vital man, he'd lost weight, his face was thin and pale, and his eyes looked glassy. 'What's wrong?' I asked. 'Nothing,' he insisted. It wasn't until after we had all spent Christmas Day together that Dad went to bed early and Mom broke the news to me. Dad had a tumor. He was going in for tests to see whether 'it' had spread. I asked Mom if 'it' meant he had cancer. She looked away as though she believed that if no one used the word 'cancer' the problem might go away.

"The next day I kept thinking, 'This couldn't have come at a worse time in my career,' for I had just been promoted to assistant producer—the first time a woman had held that position on our show. I wasn't ready for Dad's illness and all it entailed. When Mom called me with the test results, I was in shock. 'It can't be true,' I thought. Why was Dad so stubborn all those years when we tried unsuccessfully to get him to stop smoking? Crazily, I even resented my best friend, Vickie, whose father had recently gone in for tests and found out that the lump on his prostate was benign.

"Dad's cancer was so widespread the doctors advised against surgery. Offering only some unproven experimental drugs, they said he had just a few months to live. While I hated the idea of my father being used as a guinea pig, Mom insisted, 'Your father and I have talked it over with the doctors, and we feel that if there's any chance they can keep him alive, it's worth the price.'

"Since the drugs were making him vomit and lose his hair, I spent the next several days running up hundreds of dollars in phone bills searching for an alternative therapy Dad would agree to. Every time I broached the subject with Mom, she became furious. The doctors accused me of trying to get in the way of my father's treatments. My father was angry that I would even consider challenging his faith in the doctors.

"In his dreary hospital room, Dad spent most of his time asleep or in a drugged state. The few times he felt like talking were no better. His condition made him impatient and short-tempered; nearly every night he'd ask me questions like why I wasn't marrying a nice Catholic professional instead of dating my Jewish screenwriter friend. I tried to conceal my hurt feelings, but no matter what I said, it was the wrong thing. Each time I kissed my father's forehead I couldn't help thinking this might be the last time. Part of me wanted the ordeal to be over and for him to die, while deep inside I could feel myself desperately crying, 'Daddy, don't leave me.' "

When a Parent Is Dying: The Stages of Loss and Acceptance

Prior to coming in to discuss her problems, Margaret was feeling immobilized by her mixed emotions. She wanted more than anything to make contact with her father, yet she resented him for remaining stubborn and unapproachable even as he was dying. She wanted to do something to help her father and the other family members, yet she had no idea how to help herself deal with the work and personal conflicts his illness had precipitated.

During the first few weeks after finding out that her father's illness was terminal, Margaret experienced the symptoms of loss. She suffered from difficulty concentrating, a loss of appetite and sudden pangs of guilt. Her performance at work was hampered by insomnia and chronic fatigue. Her moods swung erratically: at times she was fearful, sad or irritable for no apparent reason. She had frequent conflicts with her boyfriend, sister and parents.

Margaret feared that something terrible must be wrong with her, but such symptoms are to be expected during a major emotional crisis like the terminal illness of a parent. Even if your parent lived a full life, or if the illness came as no surprise, or if your relationship was less than amicable, the potential loss of a parent is a major psychological event that should not be underestimated. Just as the body needs rest, attention and nurturance to heal an injury, so do we each need to follow a few emotional "first aid" principles to fully experience, understand and accept a parent's dying.

Even though most people assume that mourning and grief do not begin until a loved one has died, in fact the psychological stages of loss, acceptance and recovery start as soon as your parent's illness or mental deterioration begins.

Like many families facing the terminal illness of a loved one, Margaret, her father, mother and sister were individually and as a family stuck with unresolved feelings and unspoken needs. As I explained to Margaret, "In order to be of assistance to your father and the other members of your family, you first need to work through the stages of loss and acceptance yourself. Until you come to grips with the mixed feelings that are holding you back, you will be frustrated in your attempts to more deeply connect with your father and share your love with him."

I. SHOCK AND DENIAL

The first stage of dealing with an emotional loss is often marked by shock and denial. You may find yourself thinking, "Why me?" "Why did it have to happen now?" "If only the doctor had . . . ," or "If only I had . . ." In a fruitless attempt to change the past, your mind may be racing with questions about what you or your parent could have done differently. In Margaret's case, she had feelings that included "This is the wrong time," "Why couldn't Dad have stopped smoking?" and "If only he'd try one of the alternative therapies I believe in." On some mornings, she woke up "wishing it was all a bad dream and expecting to find my father healthy and active again." While she was at work, she often reported "pretending none of this was happening" and "suppressing my fears while trying to be cheerful."

No matter how you may dwell on the past or try to deny your feelings, sooner or later you will need to face up to the immediate reality of your situation. You hurt. The intensity of your pain may surprise or frighten you. You need to rest and reduce some of the other pressures in your life. Give yourself permission to take some time off from work. Call your closest friends to ask for their emotional support. Tell them if you need company or help with your shopping, baby-sitting or other everyday responsibilities. Don't be afraid to feel sad, to cry or, in private, to scream out your rage.

In many families, the seriousness of the illness is kept from the patient or from children, friends and business associates until the very end. In other cases, unrealistic promises such as "There's nothing to worry about, you're going to be fine," "You won't feel any discomfort after the operation" or "The doctors say you'll be home in no time" create more problems than they solve. While we all need hope and it is never appropriate to eliminate the possibility of a remission or an improvement, false reassurances and excessive denial elicit mistrust and alienation. As we all know from childhood, there is nothing worse than being the only person left out of a secret. Rather than making promises you might not be able to keep, you can relieve a great deal of your parent's anguish by offering things you can guarantee: that you will be his or her advocate with the doctors and hospital, that you will do everything feasible to see that the pain is lessened, and that you will be with your parent as much as possible.

During the initial shock of diagnosis, decisions and confronting painful realities, your judgment may be clouded and your energy diminished by the confusing impulses rushing through you. Your parent is in mortal danger and your family frantic. You are being asked to deal with highly complex medical information and to rearrange major priorities. Many strong and independent people become helpless and insecure when they first discover their parent is dying. Rather than fearing these inevitable feelings, you must recognize that they signify the beginning of a slow process of acceptance and recovery.

It is possible for tremendous guilt feelings and suicidal thoughts to emerge as an expression of your inner turmoil. The thoughts per se are not dangerous; they are a symptom of your pain. If you are afraid you might act on your suicidal impulses, immediately seek the help of a qualified mental health professional or go to your local hospital emergency room. As much as the emotional intensity may upset you at first, keep in mind that you *will* get better. Healing takes time. No matter how helpless, impatient or confused you may feel, remind yourself that acceptance and recovery can progress only if you fully experience each stage of grieving.

2. ANGER AND DEPRESSION

Once you begin to acknowledge the impact of your parent's illness on your emotions, you will probably go through the second stage of recovery, anger and depression. For some people, this stage of mood swings, memories and introspection is relatively brief; for others, it comes and goes for as long as your parent is ill. To deal effectively with the sadness, rage, ambivalence and inner turmoil of this stage, the following guidelines are essential:

Be with the pain. If you had suffered a broken leg, you wouldn't think twice about asking others to help nor about taking time to rest and regain your strength. Your parent is dying—give yourself permission to feel sad, cry and be alone with your memories. If you aren't willing to take care of your emotional needs as they arise, the bottled-up pain may trouble you years later. Be gentle with yourself, reaffirm your beliefs and let yourself be comforted. If the terminally ill parent is your last remaining parent, you may experience the common pain and emptiness of "Oh my God, this will mean I'm an orphan." Two of the most important people in your life will no longer be there for you. Even if it has been years since you felt dependent on your parents, the impact of losing them is nonetheless profound.

It's O.K. to feel angry. Most people believe it is wrong or disrespectful to feel anger for a parent who is dying. Anger is an expression of the loss you are suffering; the issue is dealing with this emotion effectively. You may feel anger toward your parent for becoming ill, toward the doctors or the hospital for not doing more, toward your other parent, yourself or the Fates. Sibling rivalries also tend to flare up when a parent is ill or dying. Rather than dumping your feelings on your loved ones, find a safe place to scream, cry or write out your feelings of rage. If you release the anger in these harmless ways you will avoid arguments, accidents and ulcers. The anger will dissipate as your hurt heals. Beware of venting your anger in a destructive way, such as in alcohol or drug abuse.

Living with uncertainty is never smooth. Both for the course of your parent's illness and for months after your parent has died, your moods will be subject to fluctuations. Some days you may feel positive and hopeful, only to find yourself burdened the next day by sadness, guilt or painful memories. Sundays, holidays and birthdays can be especially trying times. Depression is often worst in the mornings or if you get a cold or a bout of the flu. Rather than resisting these ups and downs, you must nurture yourself and accept that you will be emotionally vulnerable for a while.

Staying sullen and withdrawn is no proof of love. While

many people assume that facing death means you must act downtrodden and maudlin, in fact you can become closer with your family and appreciate every precious moment. You need to make a conscious decision to favor the positive under these trying circumstances. This can be a time for sharing old memories, expressing your love, asking important questions, cleaning up unfinished business, simply holding hands, or being together without any expectations or demands.

During the several weeks in which Margaret visited her father in the hospital almost every day, she dealt with her mood shifts in a variety of constructive ways. She worked through her resentments on her own. With the help of her boyfriend, she was able to cry and experience the sadness she had been holding inside. She allowed herself to admit that even though she was a successful and independent woman in her career, she was frightened at the prospect of losing her father. She began to keep a journal of her thoughts and feelings. Even though it had been years since she had used crayons or felt-tip pens, she began to draw and found the spontaneous images relaxing and therapeutic.

Instead of becoming a boring routine, Margaret's hospital visits were more satisfying once she began to read aloud to her father from newspapers, magazines or books he found interesting. According to Margaret, "I started to appreciate Dad's reminiscences about his career in politics. When I was growing up, I used to resent his stories because they were the reason he was always away from home. Politics was his world, not mine. Now I began to take pride when he would describe how he started out without an education, worked at two jobs to support his family and raised himself out of the ghetto to become a powerful figure in the Democratic Party.

I looked forward to his recollections of helping John F. Kennedy get elected and loved watching his face light up when he told, for the hundredth time, how he once said to a Supreme Court Justice, 'I've broken a few rules in my time and I'll do it again for an honest friend.' "

3. ACCEPTANCE AND UNDERSTANDING

The final stage of healing your emotional pain is marked by acceptance and understanding. Acceptance means being at peace with the illness and the inevitability of death—even though your parent might die at any time, you are appreciating each moment together. Understanding means honoring your parent's feelings and needs, as well as your own, without judgment or criticism.

Acceptance does not mean the same thing as resignation or the loss of hope. Even the most severely ill patient needs and deserves hope that an improvement is possible. Rather than defying death, acceptance allows you to experience the final days, weeks or months of your parent's life on earth with a sense of peace and quiet affection. The more you are able to let your parent go in peace, the easier it will be for him or her to tie up loose ends and reach a feeling of completion and satisfaction. For many parents, the hardest part of dying is the uncertainty that their lives were worthwhile or that their responsibilities to their children have ended. Letting your parent know how much you understand and appreciate his or her many contributions to your life is an important gift you can share.

Some people may have a tendency to bypass anger and depression and move too quickly to acceptance because of their belief in a life after death. No matter what our belief, we have to accept our human attachments and work through our feelings of loss and abandonment. Only when we do our personal mourning completely can we better appreciate the eternal aspects of life. From a transcendental perspective, death becomes not only an ending but a beginning of a whole new spiritual adventure where loved ones can remain forever united.

For many people, acceptance means no longer wishing your parent would face death in a different fashion. Quite often health professionals feel especially guilty, inadequate and resentful when their parent suffers from a painful illness, fails to work through unfinished business or experiences emotional anguish. Strong-willed individuals exhort their parent to "fight to the bitter end" or "rage against the dying of the light." While it is natural to want to "save" our parents or to want to reduce their suffering, our parents do not have to live or die according to our expectations, wishes or values.

Reaching acceptance and understanding means that you will stop wanting your parent to be different from the way he or she is. If your father is five foot eight, wishing he could be six feet tall is pointless. In a similar fashion, if you are still wishing your parents had been more open, understanding or affectionate or that they could have lived ten years longer, the time has come to accept what is and always will be. Still wanting to change, criticize and blame your parents not only is unfair to them but prevents you from being at peace with yourself as you face their imminent loss.

"What Do I Say to Him?"

As Margaret worked through her feelings in the various stages of loss, there were a number of times when she felt awkward and uncomfortable not knowing how to discuss sensitive topics with her father. Like many children of aging or dying parents, she was unsure about how to express her point of view without saying the wrong thing or getting embroiled in a conflict. As a general rule, I suggested she remember to consider her father's needs and feelings and find a way to express her viewpoints without criticizing or trying to change anyone.

For instance, Margaret was against the experimental chemotherapy that, in her view, was making her father much sicker and more uncomfortable than the cancer itself. To help her discuss the issue without attacking her father's belief in his doctors or criticizing his necessary hope for a cure, I encouraged her to be compassionate yet firm. Addressing her father, Margaret said, "Dad, the chemotherapy is experimental and according to the doctors has only a ten percent chance of prolonging life. At the same time it's producing a number of side effects, which may be shortening your life or making your remaining time very uncomfortable. The other choice you have is to stop the chemotherapy and come home with round-the-clock nursing. The choice, Dad, is up to you, and I'll be supportive of whatever decision you make. My main goal is for you to be comfortable and to know we're with you whatever happens."

Using similar empathic and nonpressuring statements, Margaret was able to help her father with a number of issues that had formerly been off limits in their relationship. Along with her mother and sister, Margaret helped her father to iron out the details of his will. They found out what he wanted for funeral arrangements and which charities his friends could support to honor him. When Margaret asked, "Is there anyone you'd like to see?" her father told her to call his older brother, whom he hadn't spoken to for more than twenty years. When the older brother flew in to see him and spent an hour alone with Margaret's father, both men were in tears.

Joy Mixed with Sorrow

Six weeks before his death, Margaret's father decided that he wanted to spend his remaining time at home, because "I want to be near my things and look out the bedroom window at my favorite view." As Margaret describes them, the last weeks were an unforgettably rewarding time. "Something changed in Dad once he got out of the hospital and returned to his sunlit bedroom. For several days, his old friends came by to see him. Each moment I was there was a chance to be close to him. Instead of resenting his idiosyncrasies, I found that his personality now became dear to me.

"When he got a phone call and was too weak to hold the receiver, I did it for him. When the private nurse needed help turning Dad or rearranging his sheets, I helped by propping him up on his side. You learn a lot about death when you experience the simple events and unspoken intimacy of watching someone learn to let go. Dying does not have to be a terrible time.

"On some afternoons he and I just stared into each other's eyes and cried. There was nothing to be said or done but love one another. We were both afraid and yet in those moments we both connected at a level beyond fear. The last few days Dad was asleep a great deal and didn't talk much. One time he opened his eyes from a daydream and asked, 'Do you know where Benton Harbor is?' I told him it was in Michigan. He smiled and said, 'Last night you and I went there in my old Packard. We took a boat out on the lake and then stopped for pizza. It was fun.' I stroked his face and smiled back at him. We both knew how much we cared.

"Even though he knew he was dying, he still kept his dreams alive. Once in the middle of a fitful sleep he opened his eyes and said, 'Meg, I'm going to write a book.' I asked him, 'What will it be about?' He answered, 'How I faced death with my wife and children.'

"Seeing how relaxed I was being with Dad, Mom began to let down some of her defenses. She and I talked late at night when everyone else was asleep. During the afternoons, when I was at work, she often sat for hours holding Dad's hand and not saying anything. Walking in and seeing them so in love was one of the richest experiences I can remember.

"After he died, my mother, sister and I sat by Dad's bedside for more than an hour before calling the funeral home. Crying together, holding each other and feeling his spirit surrounding us, we became incredibly close that day. There was so much love in that room; God was generous with us in letting us say goodbye to Dad with so much tenderness and emotion. I cried a lot the next few days and still feel waves of joy mixed with sorrow. My father taught me many things, but most important, his death taught me to appreciate the miracle of being alive. We got closer during his last few months than at any point during his life. For that I will always be grateful."

"Don't Worry About Mom"

For much of our lives we may have taken our parent(s) for granted, believing that "He (or she) will outlive us all" or that "if they need something, they'll ask." In fact, most parents are reluctant to ask their children for help. Most children find it difficult to broach the subject of finances, living arrangements, old age or death.

When children and parents fail to communicate, the result is a missed opportunity for healing their relationship. With insufficient warning, a parent dies and the surviving children are left with unfinished business, unspoken love and the inevitable guilt and remorse. To illustrate the problems that can arise in dealing with the sudden death of a parent, I asked a medical colleague to describe the feelings surrounding his mother's death. A woman who "gave everything for her children," Charles' mother had borne eleven of them, including one that died in infancy and another with cerebral palsy. As Charles remembered:

"My graduation from medical school was a gala event. Eight brothers and sisters made the trip, along with Mom and Dad. Mom was sickly, but nobody gave it much thought. 'Oh, she always acts like this,' I told my girlfriend. 'Don't worry about Mom.'

"For years Mom had been taking heart medications. Sometimes I would nag her and ask, 'Did you take your pills?' She'd just smile and say she had even if she hadn't. Mom needed to control her life in all aspects just as she needed to control each one of us. We hated her for it and we loved her for it, too. When she showed her love and affection, like when any of us was sick or hospitalized, she was golden. With a gift from God, she was a natural healer. It got to the point that each kid would get sick just to get Mom's love. In a large family there was never enough, so we all learned to seek attention in various ways. When she would complain about her heart or say she was tired, we would ignore her or tease her that she was 'like the rock of Gibraltar.'

"Then on the third day of my internship, I got a message

that she was in the hospital. In terror I called one of my sisters, then the hospital my mother was admitted to. She had just come from surgery. With tremendous control in his voice, my father told me, 'Charlie, it doesn't look good.' I said I'd be right there, hung up the phone and started to cry.

"In a panic I rushed home, picked up a change of clothes and jumped in the car for a three-hour drive at seventy miles per hour, yelling, sobbing, 'No! No! Mom, you can't do this to me. I wanted to help you. I've worked my ass off to become a doctor and now you won't even let me help you!'

"I felt so responsible for not doing enough. I had failed her when all the signs were there. It hurt to remember all the times I could have done something.

"Fortunately, I made it to the hospital in one piece and rushed into the recovery room. Mother was nowhere to be found. The nurses told me the details—saddle embolus to both iliacs, severe cerebral hypoxia with no vessels that could be used for a bypass, then renal shutdown. She had died fifteen minutes after I called.

"In a daze, I excused myself and rushed to the emergency room to see if Dad was still there. Back to pathology. 'Oh my God! Did they do an autopsy on her?' I couldn't bear to think of it. Up to medical records to review the procedures and data. Swearing at those sons of bitches. They never got any blood work on her. What was her potassium? They knew she had a heart condition!

"Then on to the home front, grieving in silence, staring, idle conversations. It was strange finding Dad so calm and in control, seeing how the business of death was a cold reality. Preparing the house, banks, closing accounts, a gravesite and tombstone, how deep to be dug and should we invest in future gravesites. The casket and how much to spend. Will we look cheap? Where will the money come from to pay for my brothers and sisters to go to college?

"I watched my father's inner turmoil as he struggled with these decisions. I watched him age in a matter of days. We all walked through it zombielike, numb, occasionally breaking through to grieve together. We protected ourselves by trying to focus on the most needed tasks at hand. 'Angela's coming in at six from Florida. Joan and Bruce will pick her up.'

"Seeing the body made me nauseated and sick. I who had done so many autopsies, dealt with death so often in my medical training, was now repelled at the fact of having to view my own mother's corpse.

"Mostly those first few days were filled with confusion, an empty feeling, sadness that she was gone, anger that she didn't say goodbye. All of us kids felt like we were part of some grandiose display for the relatives, the main attraction in a sideshow everyone was coming to see.

"Six weeks later, the phone calls to my father are still laced with loneliness. We try to resolve our guilt, our feelings of having failed her, by saying there was nothing more we could have done. Sometimes the explanations make sense; more often than not I still feel inadequate to understand her or accept that she is gone.

"I remember her telling me how she lived for motherhood, saying, 'My life is my kids; I'll live and I'll die for them.' Then with tears rolling down her face, she'd lament, 'Don't tell me that I'm unhappy. All that I want is to see my children grow up healthy and successful.'

"Mentally, physically, emotionally, this family consumed all that could be given from one individual. If only I had one final chance to thank her, to appreciate her, to tell her, 'Mom, I love you.' "

Recovering from a Parent's Sudden, Unexpected Death

We go through stages of loss and acceptance when a parent dies suddenly similar to those when a parent is seriously ill or dying. When he first heard the news of his mother's death, Charles was in shock. Rushing through the medical records, he tried to find something the doctors had failed to do. He was angry at the doctors, at his mother and especially at himself for not doing more. His mood shifts and depression began during the funeral and affected him to varying degrees over the next several months.

Even though Charles got back to work after only a few days, he soon discovered that the process of healing takes longer. Just when he thought his grief was over, mementos or familiar situations would trigger insecure and grief-filled moments. He tried to hold his feelings inside, but soon found he needed to share his pain with his girlfriend and a medical colleague.

In addition to the sadness and regret you experience, recovering from the loss of a parent is an opportunity to appreciate the gifts he or she gave you. By honoring the best in your parents, you keep their spirit alive and continue the contribution they made to you and the other people they touched. The roots, traditions and ethnic heritage they passed on to you may take on additional meaning after they are gone. The beliefs and values they held may become more understandable and worthwhile as you view their lives from a broader perspective.

A helpful experience for Charles was to go through the letters, pictures and mementos that, of necessity, needed to be sorted out. Instead of sticking all the boxes in a closet because going through them is painful or time-consuming, you can use this task as an opportunity to rediscover your parent and appreciate the fact that he or she may have saved many of your letters, childhood drawings or long-forgotten gifts.

On the other hand, you should be careful not to become tyrannized by the common desire of many surviving children to do everything "exactly as Mom [or Dad] would want me to do." Instead of trying to overcompensate for the past, you need to accept that what's done is done. You cannot bring back your parent, nor can you win his or her forgiveness by excessive striving or anxious attempts to fulfill unmet demands.

For the first several months after his mother died, Charles found himself "working insanely hard at my internship. As if to prove to Mom that I'd made the right decision, I was killing myself taking on more duties than I could handle." The sudden death of a parent may force you to reexamine your priorities. If you have been pursuing a career, marriage or lifestyle for your parent's sake, you will now be faced with the question of what *you* really want. If you had always perceived yourself as sheltered, naïve or carefree, the death of one or both parents may radically alter your outlook on life. On the other hand, you may find decisions involving personal growth are spurred by the crisis of a parent's death. During this period, while your judgment is clouded, you should think twice before making any major changes. In many cases, a parent's death will force you to look more closely at your feelings about marriage and divorce, having children, changing careers, and making a larger commitment to your health and loved ones.

To accept your parent's death includes being at peace with both the happy and the sad times you shared. Understanding the impact of your parent's life and death may include discovering how your conflicts helped you become a stronger and more capable human being. While some people remember only the bitter disputes and others block out everything but the good times, making peace with your departed parent allows you to learn from all the experiences in your relationship and to grow as an individual.

Letting Go of the "If Only's"

Just as Charles felt a number of regrets about his mother's death, each of us, to a greater or lesser extent, feels guilty when a parent dies. If your mother died in childbirth, if one or both of your parents died when you were young, or if you felt in any way responsible for contributing to the illness or accident that resulted in your parent's death, you may be carrying inside you tremendous feelings of regret. Even if your parent died after a long and full life, you may be harboring guilt feelings for things you did or failed to do.

Some people seem to hold on to unresolved feelings toward a departed parent "out of respect." In fact, to fully love, respect and fondly remember your parent, you must unravel the sorrow, shame and disappointments you harbor. Working through your guilt and regrets requires letting go of the "if only's" that prevent you from making peace with your mother or father.

Following my instructions, Charles prepared for this exercise by setting aside an hour of complete privacy. Unplugging the phones and putting a Do Not Disturb sign on the door of his study, he sat down with a pen and pad of paper, a box of tissues and a series of old photographs and mementos of his mother. Since most people find this to be an emotional exercise, you should make sure to give yourself enough time and privacy to fully work through your feelings. For most, the exercise takes from thirty minutes to an hour and should be repeated a few times or whenever excessive guilt disrupts your peace of mind.

As though writing a letter to your parent, list the regrets you feel about your relationship with him or her. Regrets are defined as the things you did or failed to do that leave you feeling guilty or remorseful. Included in your regrets are the things you would like to have told your parent while he or she was alive. For many, these memories come easily. In some cases, however, regrets are deeply submerged and take time to be released. That's why it's valuable to do this exercise a number of times.

The regrets exercise is helpful for letting go of the "if only's" not only with a recently departed parent but also with one that died many years or decades earlier. Having the opportunity to work through the guilt, resolve any lingering conflicts and express your unspoken appreciation is of great psychological benefit. Sometimes a flood of emotion will come up, while other times it may appear that "nothing much happened." Either way there is value in doing the exercise.

Charles found that looking at a photograph of his mother and himself when he was a small child helped him remember feelings and incidents he thought he had long forgotten. As he began to write out his list of regrets, Charles described feeling "an incredible release. Tears started streaming down my face and I just kept writing. There were so many things I wanted to tell my mother that I never had the courage or the chance to say."

Among the regrets Charles wrote were the following:

Dear Mom,

I regret that we had an argument the last time we saw each other.

I regret never having a chance to say goodbye.

I regret not being there when you died.

I regret the worries I caused you all those nights in high school when I didn't come home and didn't bother to call.

I regret the times I forgot to call or write on your birthday.

I regret the time I embarrassed you in church by laughing during the sermon.

I regret that you didn't live to see me get married.

I regret that I never gave you any grandchildren.

I regret that you and I never were able to just spend a day together as friends.

I regret that you aren't here now to comfort me.

The more specific the regrets, the more they will release the pain you feel. Your goal in this exercise is not to dwell on your guilt or criticize yourself. Holding on to your sadness and pain is an inappropriate way to respect and honor your parent. Instead of continuing to punish yourself, this exercise will help you to forgive yourself as part of loving and appreciating your parent.

By sharing his list with his girlfriend and one of his brothers, Charles was able to break through the emotional isolation he had felt since his mother's death. His brother, who was also plagued by guilt, benefited from having the chance to air his own regrets. Charles and his girlfriend became much closer once he was able to explain the feelings he had about his mother and the moods he had been experiencing since her death.

Giving Yourself Compassion

It is essential that you experience being forgiven for your regrets. A powerful means for completing the "if only's" with your parent is to visualize or imagine your mother or father hearing your regrets, understanding your feelings and then expressing his or her forgiveness. Close your eyes and visualize your parent listening, smiling, comforting you and saying, "I forgive you" as you share your list of regrets. You might also imagine your parent stroking your face, holding your hand, giving you a hug or in some other way acknowledging you.

If you have trouble imagining your parent, look at an old photograph and share the regrets with his or her image, until you have the inner sense of your parent understanding and accepting your love. Once again, the goal of this exercise is not to punish yourself by lingering over old conflicts. By consciously visualizing your parent accepting your apologies and receiving your love, you will be able to release any remaining guilt from your system.

As an additional way to complete your mourning, think for a moment about the words or feelings you always wanted from your parent but never got. What special acknowledgment, compliment or statement of love and support were you always hoping your parent would give you? What did you always wish to hear that would allow you to feel more whole and complete? Close your eyes and imagine your parent saying or doing, a number of times, what you most sought. Give yourself several such "treatments." Feel the relief that comes from finally being understood and appreciated by your parent.

As an example, Charles imagined his mother telling him the words he had always wished she would say. With his eyes closed, he described seeing his mother's face and hearing her tell him, "Charlie, don't work so hard. Be happy. I love you." Using that visualization a number of times, Charles allowed himself to experience his mother's forgiveness. He discovered that he no longer had to feel guilty for her death. Nor did he have to continue on an endless treadmill to win her or anyone else's approval. According to Charles, "I'm still highly motivated but less driven. I no longer do to me what I saw my mother doing to herself and her kids. Since I'm no longer killing myself to win her approval, I feel closer to her than ever."

7

Becoming Your Own Best Parent

When you were a small child, the responsibility for your health and happiness rested with your parents. An infant cannot feed, clothe or comfort itself. A young child cannot survive, physically or emotionally, without the help of others. As a result of being totally dependent, you had to learn to act in a manner that would get other people to do what you could not do for yourself. You discovered how to cry when you were hungry, to pout when you were upset, to be stubborn when you didn't get your way and to act cute when you wanted someone's attention.

As adults, we retain basic psychological needs for nurturance, encouragement and affection. Most of us believe that the responsibility for satisfying these needs rests outside of us: if we are in a bad mood at home, we blame our partner; when we feel frustrated at work, we blame our boss or "the system" ; when we see something we don't like in ourselves, we are apt to blame our parents for "making us that way."

As adults we may use more subtle methods than a child's pouts and outbursts, but we do have ways to look to others to give us what we refuse to give ourselves. How often have you used shrugged shoulders, a victimized expression on your face or complaints to get someone to feel sorry for you and take care of your problem? How often have you pretended you couldn't do something when in fact you could but didn't want to? How often have you waited for external circumstances to force you to act rather than choosing for yourself?

Even though it may be years since you stopped depending on your parents for your sustenance, decisions and affection, you may still be secretly wishing that they or someone else (a Sugar Daddy, an Earth Mother, a Prince Charming or a Miracle) would come to your rescue. Rather than taking charge of your life and living up to your potential, you may be waiting for someone to do it for you and resenting that no one does.

Crucial to making peace with your parents is discovering that you are responsible for your own health and happiness. As an adult, you have the opportunity to become your own best nurturer, coach and guide—the one you may have been looking for elsewhere. Instead of complaining about the ways your parents didn't live up to your expectations, you can learn to give yourself what you've been missing.

Nurturing Yourself

Many people treat themselves like criminals. Creating far more criticism and disapproval than their parents ever gave them, these individuals go through life afraid to take risks, unable to give themselves credit and aware only of their failures and shortcomings.

When you are fearful or upset, do you give yourself the loving "I'm on your side" encouragement of a nurturing parent or the disapproving "Stop being so sensitive" rejection of a critical parent? When you suffer a disappointment or setback, do you tell yourself, "I love you anyway and there will be another chance," or do you reprimand yourself with comments like "See, I knew you couldn't do it," "Who are you trying to fool?" or "Better quit while you're ahead" ? Undoubtedly you internalized from your parents a mixed bag of both nurturing and critical attitudes. You now have the opportunity to more consciously become the type of parent for yourself that you need.

By nurturing yourself, I do not mean becoming a self-indulgent hedonist who must say yes to every desire. Quite often nurturing yourself means saying no to self-destructive habits, such as procrastination, drug abuse, alcoholism or chronic self-criticism. Growth includes the integration of seemingly opposite values. Unrestricted license more often than not produces chaos and frustration; to be fulfilled means integrating freedom within self-imposed limits. The art of self-restraint, setting limits with understanding and enjoyment, is a crucial part of self-parenting and a way we can demonstrate how much we care for ourselves. Self-nurturance can mean giving yourself a well-deserved day off, eating more nutritious food or giving yourself encouragement in your work. It can mean forgiving yourself for an unfortunate mistake or volunteering your services to others.

Personal growth does not come as a result of self-hate. If you have been trying to lose weight because you can't stand the way you look and hate yourself every time you get on the scale, any weight loss will inevitably be short-lived. A week or a month later the pounds will be back. Self-hate undermines the best of intentions in a self-fulfilling prophecy.

The paradox of personal growth is that you have to learn to love yourself exactly as you are as a basis for lasting positive change. Instead of your life being tied up in self-hate, your energy is free to support yourself in making the changes you prefer. Your entire self-worth does not depend on your decision to lose twenty pounds. Loving yourself, with a balance of acceptance and self-discipline, is crucial to maintaining your ideal weight through proper nutrition, stress reduction and exercise.

Taking Charge

Even though you may know intuitively that you alone are responsible for your well-being and that you need to be more nurturing of yourself, knowing and doing something about it are two very different things. For many people, the habits of looking outside themselves for appreciation and support are deeply ingrained. As much as they promise "I'll start today," they soon revert to the avoidance of making decisions and instead wait anxiously to be rescued. As much as they realize "I need to make some changes in my life," they are immobilized by their own self-criticism and fear of taking the first step.

Since personal growth comes from accepting and appreciating yourself exactly as you are at every step along the path to your goal, you will have to make peace with even the lazy, petty parts of yourself you hide and don't want anyone to know about. We all have those sides to us; welcome to the human race. If you resist your petty or dark side it is more likely to persist and run you. By accepting all of yourself, you are better able to accept the human weaknesses of others.

"I Had to Stop Running"

Becoming your own best parent is an enormous challenge for most of us. The case of Teri, a thirty-year-old fashion designer, demonstrates the various steps you must take to bridge the gap from *knowing* that you are responsible for yourself to *doing* what it takes to make that a reality.

Teri had grown up in a family of four children in a suburb of Detroit, and she describes how "I never had the sense that there was anything deficient about my upbringing. My parents told us often how much they loved us. We children seemed healthy and normal, got good grades and never caused any serious trouble. The last thing I ever expected was that any of us would wind up going to a therapist."

When Teri first came to see me, her life was in turmoil. Her employer had filed for bankruptcy and laid off Teri and the other designers. Her second marriage was in trouble and Teri had just found out that she was pregnant. As she saw it, "I couldn't imagine bringing a child into this world. How could I take care of someone else when I was doing such a rotten job taking care of myself?"

Teri was chronically tense, with frequent headaches and an inability to fall asleep at night. Her emotional strain had been increasing for a number of years. According to Teri, "Everything seemed fine the first few years after I moved from Detroit to New York, studied fashion design and got married. But the marriage didn't last—he wanted me to mother him and I wanted him to take care of me. I remember flying home then and really looking at Mom when she came to the airport, as if seeing her for the first time. She was chubby and good-natured, and all my friends used to love her, but as I went up to her, my heart dropped. I felt the coldness that had grown up between us over the last few years, and I knew there would be no hug or kiss, no words of comfort. The barrier we had both put up years before meant that all we could exchange was meaningless gossip.

"I asked myself, 'Doesn't she even care why I'm here? Doesn't she have any idea what I'm feeling?' I was terrified about being alone after my divorce. I wanted someone to talk to, yet I realized that Mom was not the right person. What I wanted and couldn't get was the plain and simple mother love that I thought ought to be natural between mother and daughter. I began to tell her of the pain I was feeling, but as soon as I started to talk, I heard the familiar 'Teri, you've got to control yourself. You're fine. There's no need to be upset.'

"Control is the word for it. Mom had a tight lid on her feelings and always made sure we looked and acted like happy little children, her perfect brood. I was too upset to live with my mother's control. After only a few hours in Detroit, I told her I had to fly back to New York. I had gone home for some understanding, but all I got was how I 'should' feel."

Teri found a new job with a women's clothing maker in Los Angeles and, after a number of short-lived romances, remarried at the age of twenty-nine. She had "high hopes that this time, in Cliff, I'd found the right man," but their arguments and mistrust had increased to the point that they were considering a separation after only eighteen months. Then with the loss of her job and the discovery that she was pregnant, Teri had "reached the point where I had to stop running. I couldn't keep pretending everything was going to get better as soon as I found the right job or the right husband. I was terrified of being alone again, but I didn't know what to do to take charge of my life."

How Do You Treat Yourself?

Like many of us, Teri had never discovered how to become her own best parent. She couldn't learn it from her mother because her mother was herself unfulfilled, living only through her husband and her children. Her father was also of little help. Though he was successful in business, he was afraid of his feelings and depended on Teri's mother to bolster him. Teri's second husband couldn't lead her life for her either. As much as she resisted, Teri had to learn how to nurture herself to experience more satisfaction in her life.

To illustrate the importance of self-nurturance, examine the attitudes you hold about yourself. Most of us are much harsher on ourselves than we need to be. For instance, do you often feel embarrassed when someone compliments you? When you look in the mirror, do you always find something to criticize about the way you look? Do you often inconvenience yourself by saying, "Sure, I'll do it for you," when you wish you had said no? Are you shy or reluctant about admitting your strengths? Do you often refuse to let yourself relax, have fun or receive credit because you think you don't deserve it? By beginning to recognize the self-punishing habits you acquired as a child, you can change these into self-nurturing traits.

As an example, Teri successfully came to grips with the crises in her life by mastering the following principles.

Principles of Self-Parenting

SEEING PROBLEMS AS OPPORTUNITIES

Many people assume "I'd be happy if only I could get rid of these problems." In fact, once you solve one set of challenges you will inevitably be faced by others. Your perspective is the key: life is meant to be challenging. Rather than overwhelming you, problems can be turned into opportunities.

Even though Teri had had the courage to move to New York when she was eighteen, had been successful as a clothing designer and was independent enough to leave her first marriage, she still described herself as a "scared little girl inside, always hoping my world isn't going to collapse like a house of cards." Part of becoming your own best parent is learning how to be there for yourself when your fears, doubts or resistances come up. Instead of being immobilized by the challenges in your life, use anxiety as a stimulus to growth. Rather than hoping that someone else will find the right words to comfort and encourage you, you can be that person yourself. You are not "hopelessly alone" in your troubles; you can feel aided and appreciated by the gifts of love you give yourself. This includes giving yourself at least the same understanding you would give your closest friend.

AFFIRMING YOURSELF

One of the most powerful methods for overcoming fear and developing inner strength is through the practice of affirmations. You can break through your negative beliefs about yourself, change fearful attitudes and give yourself the best "mother love" you may or may not have gotten from your parents. Affirmations are done for a few minutes each day, as well as whenever you are feeling anxious or unhappy.

For instance, Teri began to write the following affirmations several times every morning for a number of weeks. Note that in each case, she wrote the affirmation out first as an "I-statement" as if proclaiming it herself, then as a "you-statement" as if being told the affirmation by someone else, and finally as a "she-statement" as if overhearing what someone else had to say about her. Getting these affirmations from these three points of view will assist you to make these self-nurturing traits a reality. Some of the affirmations Teri wrote are:

"I Teri deserve to be loved."
"You Teri deserve to be loved."
"Teri deserves to be loved."

"I Teri can take care of myself."
"You Teri can take care of yourself."
"Teri can take care of herself."

"I Teri am the best parent I could ever ask for."
"You Teri are the best parent you could ever ask for."
"Teri is the best parent she could ever ask for."

Affirmations can also be done out loud. Whenever Teri faced a difficult challenge, she would stand in front of the mirror and say, "Teri, I have confidence in you. You are beautiful, loving and strong." Affirmations can help keep you in touch with your most positive inner voice.

DOING LESS TO ACCOMPLISH MORE

For many people, taking the first step is always the hardest. The more they procrastinate in doing something for themselves, the more they beat themselves up with self-criticism. Break down your major projects into small, manageable portions and start each day with short tasks you give yourself credit for accomplishing. Instead of criticizing yourself and always feeling "I can't be satisfied until all the work is done," acknowledge each small success by letting yourself know what you are doing right.

Prior to therapy, Teri was always in a hurry, never had enough energy and found it difficult to relax and unwind. Like many of us, she discovered that by chronically straining she actually accomplished less. At the end of each day she found herself rushing frantically but not meeting her goals.

As a result of learning to combine self-discipline with self-nurturance, she began to reduce her stress and increase the productivity in each day. Instead of incurring anxiety by placing unrealistic demands upon herself and tight scheduling, Teri made sure to leave at least an hour a day of unscheduled time for new things that came up, unexpected delays or more time to rest and unwind. She also learned to take breaks when she felt fatigued or strained. Each of us needs to combine rest and work in daily cycles that keep us from getting "burnt out." To help herself have more energy and to maintain her health during her pregnancy, Teri took TM and set aside twenty minutes before breakfast and dinner for meditation.

By "putting her nose to the grindstone," Teri had been depriving herself of the things she enjoyed. Once she began to listen to her favorite jazz music, fill her environment with plants and colorful paintings, and drink hot spiced teas while she worked, she enjoyed fashion designing again. The point to life is not just your achievements but to enjoy what you are doing.

Teri also managed to take long walks several times a week, swim at a nearby pool, attend an aerobics class for expectant mothers and start exchanging massages with her husband. As Teri described her change of attitude, "I used to put everything and everyone ahead of me, and I found I had no time to take care of myself. Now I relax more, argue less and have more energy for work and my marriage."

NURTURING ALL OF YOU

One of the benefits of becoming your own best parent is that you don't have to wait hoping for someone else to satisfy your needs. We are each complex and multifaceted individuals. Too often when we wait for others to take care of us we wind up neglecting important parts of our personality.

In Teri's case, she discovered that in addition to her work, marriage and health, she wanted to satisfy her intellectual, spiritual and friendship needs. This meant taking time to sit down with a good book, having lunch with her female friends, and attending personal growth workshops and spiritual retreats. Rather than feeling locked into a routine or cut off from her interests, Teri found that she could constantly revitalize herself and increase her enthusiasm for life by seeing that her personal needs got met.

Giving Birth to Yourself

During the nine months in which Teri was pregnant, she changed from being a person who was constantly overwhelmed by her external circumstances to feeling more content and in charge of her life. Her freelance income from fashion design increased to the extent that she no longer needed to be away from home in order to make a good living.

Her relationship with her husband became intimate and deeply committed. Her health improved even as she faced the physical challenges of pregnancy. According to Teri, "I was giving birth not only to an adorable infant but to myself as well."

As a new parent, Teri had a number of important breakthroughs with her own mother: "Having my own child helped me to appreciate the strengths in my mother. Sure she has her faults, but don't we all? Being a parent is an enormous responsibility and I'd have to say now that on the whole my mother did a terrific job.

"I've also begun to notice that what I used to perceive as her controlling me is simply her way of showing affection and concern. Sometimes it seems like she's making a lot of demands, but in truth she isn't really asking for all that much from me. She just wants to know that I love her, that I respect her viewpoint, that I'll remember her birthday and that I understand her concern for my well-being. It used to feel like a burden. Now, even with our occasional disagreements and tense moments, there's a real trust between us. Not needing her to give me the mother love I now can give myself, I appreciate her and can tell her that I love her. As a result, I am getting more love in return."

"Wait Until You Have Kids"

Conflicts you had with your parents may reappear in the conflicts you have with your children. You or your partner may find yourself resenting your children for having comforts and liberties you never had as a child. For instance, how many times have you heard yourself or another parent say "I never got away with *that* when I was a kid," "You think

I'm strict? You don't know what that word means" or "My parents couldn't afford any of the things you take for granted from me" ? If you find yourself having these types of resentments, it is a signal not necessarily to take back what you genuinely want to give your children but to reexamine some of the guilt and resentments you acquired from your own parents. The more you learn how to nurture and take care of yourself, the less you will resent the advantages given to your children.

Quite often couples set for themselves unrealistic expectations that they will "never make the same mistakes" as their parents. By overcompensating with their children for what they did not get from their parents or by swinging to the opposite extreme in matters of discipline and style, they may inadvertently create more problems than they solve.

Many parents, on the other hand, are shocked to discover that they are doing to their children just what they resented their parents having done to them. If your parents were physically violent with you, you may be finding it difficult to control your anger and to avoid acting upon your violent impulses with your children. If your parents were overly controlling, moralistic or strict, you may resent yourself or your partner for using similar devices on your children. If you couldn't stand the fights and shouting when you were a child, you may be doubly incensed by the struggles you have with your children.

Sometimes the arrival of children may cause you to start resenting your spouse by reminding you of your mother or father. When a wife is taking care of a newborn baby, it is common for the husband to relive ambivalence toward his mother. When a husband is generous or affectionate with his children, a wife often reexperiences her anger about the attention she didn't get from her father. When either parent is disciplining a child, the other partner may become enraged at how much the discipline style resembles his or her childhood traumas.

The following case demonstrates how becoming your own best parent is essential to healing childhood conflicts that reappear when you become a parent.

"I'm No Better Than My Old Man"

A partner in a law firm specializing in corporate litigation, Roger was forty years old when he first got married. His wife, Eileen, an attractive divorced mother of two teenage sons, had at one time been an amateur tennis star. After their honeymoon in Hawaii, Roger and Eileen purchased a new home for themselves and Eileen's thirteen- and sixteen-year-old sons. Yet within six months after the wedding, their "happy family" was in serious trouble.

As Roger described the problem, "I wanted to marry Eileen. That part was easy. Unfortunately, the kids came with the package. From the very beginning they did everything in their power to make life difficult for me. Maybe it was competition for Eileen's attention or maybe they just didn't like me. In any case, after working hard five and sometimes six days a week, I needed to relax at home. I like to watch football on Sundays, but when her sons would have their friends over, it was so noisy I could barely hear the set. Some nights I would come home late from the office and go to the refrigerator to make a sandwich or have a glass of milk. I could never find anything until I went into their bedrooms and found food and milk rotting on their desks. To make matters worse, when I laid the law down those brats would go crying to their mother."

Soon Roger's battles with Eileen's sons became battles with her. According to Roger, "No matter whether they were right or wrong, she defended them. She told me I was being a bigger baby than they were and accused me of harboring bad feelings toward her kids. You're damn right I had bad feelings. Those little monsters were driving me crazy, and you can bet they knew exactly what they were up to."

When Roger and I began to explore his memories of childhood, similarities to his present situation appeared. Just as Roger had always felt that his younger brothers "stole" his mother's affection away from him, so did he resent the competition for Eileen's affection. Just as Roger had rebelled against his father's angry outbursts about his "messy room," so was Roger becoming dictatorial about the boys' rooms. As Roger lamented, "For years I avoided getting married and starting a family because I couldn't imagine being a parent. When I wound up playing the role of 'Dad' for Eileen's kids, I swore I'd do it right. Now it looks as though I'm no better than my old man."

Retraining Yourself

To help Roger stop repeating the conflicts he experienced as a child, I suggested he reassess what makes for "good parenting" and start to be less anxious and more nurturing with himself and his stepsons. As I explained, *"We tend to criticize in our children what we are most critical of in ourselves."* Roger was an extremely self-critical and highly disciplined individual. The same "either do it this way or else" demands he had resented from his father were the demands he had used on himself for years. Now when he tried to set limits for his stepsons with that same tone, they felt obligated to rebel. I suggested to Roger, "As you start becoming less critical of yourself, you can become more supportive and encouraging of your stepsons as well."

Becoming a more nurturing parent for yourself and your children requires learning new emotional skills, which can be mastered much like training yourself in sports or at work. For instance, when you train yourself to improve your tennis serve, you need to have specific instructions and then practice. At first, practicing a new emotional skill may feel awkward or "not me," much like attempting your new serve. There is a tendency for the old habits to reappear, and so you need to coach and supervise yourself through the transition. With practice, you lose your self-consciousness and the new behavior becomes completely natural.

To help Roger discover the parental style that suited him, I suggested the following exercises, which you can do whether or not you have children:

I. REEXAMINING YOUR UPBRINGING

This exercise is to uncover the qualities and discipline styles you resented in your parents, as well as those you liked. By consciously looking at the role-modeling you received from your parents, you will finally be able to choose for yourself how best to guide, support and nurture yourself and your children.

Unplug the phones, put a "Do Not Disturb" sign on the door, relax and give yourself at least thirty minutes to explore the negative and positive qualities that were modeled for you as a child. Begin by describing in vivid detail the things your parents did that made you feel rejected, belittled or unloved. What messages and examples of "being a parent" did you find harmful or ineffective?

To help you remember specific traits that you perceived as unloving, look at a photograph of your parents from when you were a child and recall incidents when you needed them and they failed to communicate their love. For instance, when Roger did this exercise he remembered

"When I used to ask my father questions about business, he always told me I was too young to understand. By the time I was 'old enough,' I had already left home and was on my own."

"When I would come home from kindergarten, the first thing my mother would ask is, 'Did you behave yourself today?' She cared more about how I appeared to others than whether I had a nice day."

"One time I broke my father's favorite screwdriver and I rushed in to apologize. But when he hit me and called me 'stupid' I made up my mind never to admit to him when I made a mistake. From then on I never let myself be vulnerable with him, or probably with anyone else."

As a result of this first step, Roger became aware of a number of ways he could be a better parent for himself and his stepsons. Instead of stifling his own or their curiosity by holding the attitude "You're too young" or "Mind your own business," he decided to be more readily available to them. Instead of interrogating his stepsons about their behavior and keeping his affection for them a secret, Roger promised himself he would be less critical and more forgiving.

Next, Roger examined those times when he felt most loved by his parents. In this part of the exercise, you are to recall those times when you felt appreciated, encouraged and special. What did your parents do that made you feel loved? By what means did they convey that you could trust and respect each other? What specific qualities of being a parent did you admire in your mother and father? What things do you miss most from your childhood relationship with your parents? Recall a time when your parents taught you something constructive or shared a memorable moment with you.

While many people have trouble with this portion of the exercise, even those with very painful memories manage to recall positive traits about their parents. The more you are able to let go of your resentments and remember the ways in which you felt loved and appreciated, the more you will be able to incorporate those traits into your own parenting style. After looking at a photograph of his parents, Roger's memories included the following:

"On Sunday mornings my father would take me shopping with him to the bakery and delicatessen and then we would come home and make brunch. He would always ask me how school was that week and how I was doing. Dad was so proud when I went to law school."

"I felt loved when my mother would close her eyes and pray at the dinner table. It was a feeling of specialness that we could share a meal together."

"I felt loved when my parents drove hundreds of miles to see me play high school basketball. It meant a lot to me that they came to see me play."

2. FINDING POSITIVE ROLE MODELS

Besides your own parents, there are many opportunities for learning about what makes for good parenting. Dozens of books and articles are written each year about how to resolve conflicts, avoid communication problems and encourage love and joy within the family. Also, you can learn from the best parenting styles among your friends and relatives.

For instance, as a result of his upbringing, Roger had always believed that "when you say something once and the kids don't listen, the next time start yelling." As a result, whenever he didn't gain the cooperation of his stepsons after one request, Roger tended to get angry and hostile to "show them who's boss."

While spending a camping weekend with close friends, Roger saw repeatedly how his friends made an effort to patiently explain what they wanted two, three and sometimes four times to their children. They would find a way to explain their preferences so that their teenagers could understand and cooperate. He saw it actually took less time than yelling. Roger described the change in his behavior as a result: "I don't need to blow up and cause the kids to be rebellious and defiant. Instead of playing the tough guy all the time, I'm starting to reach them in a way they can accept."

3. WEEKLY FAMILY MEETINGS

Running a family is in some ways like running a business. If the principals don't meet regularly, chaos will ensue. Too often when they do meet it's because of conflicts that result from this lack of communication. Regular weekly meetings are important for a family or business to operate effectively. Instead of being crisis-oriented, these meetings can *focus on what individuals are doing right,* reviewing each person's needs and preventing unnecessary problems.

At my suggestion, Roger began the first family meeting by describing the purpose of getting together. Addressing both children, Roger stated with affection, "The truth is that initially we didn't ask to be thrown together. I didn't choose you guys and you didn't choose me. Because I loved your mother and you were her children, nature threw us in the same lifeboat. It would have been nice if we'd acknowledged that to each other from the beginning and then started to work together as a family. I'd like to hear your feelings about us having been thrown together . . . Instead of making life miserable for one another, let's see how each of us can begin to make it more satisfying."

To help Roger and his stepsons, I suggested the following exercise for improving cooperation in any family. Each of us has preferences about how we want others to talk to us to gain our cooperation. If they ask for our assistance one way, we gladly go along. If they ask another way, we resist or rebel. Each person is asked to describe the words and actions that make them want to cooperate and those that make them more likely to rebel. For instance, Roger began by saying

"I feel like cooperating when Eileen or anyone else asks me in a pleasant voice and waits to hear if I have any objections."

"I feel like rebelling when anyone starts by blaming me for something and makes me feel like I've done something wrong."

Eileen's elder son shared the following:

"I feel like cooperating when I don't think you're laying a power trip on me."

"I feel like rebelling when I think you're acting superior or that you don't care how I feel."

At that first meeting, Roger declared that he would be more affectionate and less quick-tempered with the boys. He also requested that they tell him directly whenever they were upset with his actions rather than complaining behind his back to Eileen or doing indirect things to get back at him. The meeting ended on a positive note with an exchange of hugs.

While I had advised Roger and Eileen not to expect changes overnight, I suggested that "the sooner you implement principles that are fair to all, the sooner your sons will cooperate. In addition to being more empathic about their needs, you must also be more specific as to what agreements each of you and the boys are willing to make in order to have a happier and more smoothly running household."

At the second meeting, Roger, Eileen and their two sons made a list of chores and responsibilities each was willing to follow. From then on, each weekly meeting began with a discussion of "The agreements I kept this week are . . ." ; "The agreements I broke this week are . . ." ; and "The changes I'm making so that I can keep all my agreements for next week are . . ."

At every weekly meeting they went around the circle sharing two things they appreciated about each person during the past week. In very specific ways this helped keep the atmosphere loving and supportive. While occasional conflicts still arose, the level of trust and affection grew.

Making a Difference

Becoming your own best parent is not a final destination but a new beginning. You can live your life with more inner peace instead of being controlled by unresolved conflicts from your upbringing. Taking charge of your life will give you more energy and vitality to express your own special talents more effectively.

Diane's case illustrates how self-parenting is a key element to reaching your goals and enjoying your life. A forty-two-year-old divorced mother, Diane entered psychotherapy because of problems she was having with her mother and her rebellious fifteen-year-old daughter, Alison. In addition, she felt as if she were "stuck in a dead-end job and still waiting for a Prince Charming to come sweep me off my feet."

Diane felt resentful and unappreciated: "I bend over backward to take care of my mother and still she says I'm not doing enough. With the men I'm attracted to, I work frantically hard to make them happy so that they'll want to be with me. Yet the more I do for them, the less they do for me. With my daughter it's the same problem. She has no initiative; I have to breathe down Alison's neck for her to do her homework."

As I explained to Diane, *"Quite often the way our loved ones treat us is a mirror of the way we treat ourselves.* The question is not whether they appreciate you, but whether you have learned to appreciate yourself. Do you choose satisfaction or do you remain chronically dissatisfied with your life in the hope that Prince Charming will recognize your plight and come to your rescue? Instead of blaming your mother, daughter or a lover for not appreciating you, it may be time for you to take charge of your life and choose to be satisfied without waiting for anyone else to do it for you."

I told Diane that I'm a psychiatrist who is not a "shrink" but a "stretch." True joy in life comes from choosing satisfaction and learning to serve others. To help Diane get started, I suggested the following assignment: "During the next week, find some way you could be of service to others without feeling burdened, unappreciated or resentful. Choose a local, human-scale problem, set specific objectives and put your energies to the test. The idea is to shrink your problems by stretching your capacities."

The next week Diane came in with the following proposal: "I love pets and little children. I have this idea that retarded children would benefit tremendously if I went around with a van full of pets and let the kids interact with the furry small animals. If they can love and hug a baby animal, they can develop more self-esteem and physical awareness skills." During the next six months, Diane worked in her spare time developing her idea into a successful enterprise that soon captivated the hearts of hundreds of retarded children and won the acceptance of dozens of school administrators.

As Diane described it proudly, "I raised twenty-five thousand dollars at a fund-raising event, and a pet-food company wants me to make this my full-time job. The more I trust myself to do things that have meaning for me, the more I'm learning to deal effectively with the other challenges in my life. I don't seem to attract selfish or shallow men any longer now that I feel good about myself. Also, my daughter Alison is more helpful and self-sufficient.

"With my mother, I noticed a great shift in my feelings for her last month on her birthday. For years I used to spend the longest time in front of the racks at the greeting card store searching for the 'right' birthday card. If it was too flowery or affectionate I knew I couldn't give it to her. If the card said 'I love you, Mom,' I felt too resentful to want to choose it. I kept looking for a simple, unemotional card that just said 'Happy Birthday,' without making me lie about my ambivalence.

"Since I have worked through my resentments and made peace with my inner parent, my mother seems very different to me. Sure, she still makes demands, but that's just her way of expressing her love. I can now receive her advice without feeling I have to comply. I know how to say 'no' when I need to and enjoy saying 'yes' when we both want to get together. She's become very excited about my business and is my number one cheerleader. She is helping me expand from reaching hundreds of kids to reaching thousands.

"This time I didn't have to send her the most unaffectionate and cautious birthday card I could find. Instead, I decided to make my own card for her to convey how much I really care. One Saturday morning I thoroughly enjoyed designing the most beautiful card I could imagine. I enclosed some heartwarming photos of us together through the years. Inside the card I wrote a special note:

" 'Dear Mom, I thought it was time I tell you some of the things I deeply appreciate about you!'

"On my list I had a dozen specific acknowledgments of her, including:

" 'I love it when you spend time with Alison. She thinks you're fun and learns a lot from your stories and the places you take her. You're a terrific grandmother.'

" 'I'm grateful that you believed in me even when I didn't believe in myself, like when I lost my job and you loaned me money.'

" 'I'm grateful for all the times you made me very special home-cooked meals. When I was sick, your chicken soup worked miracles.'

" 'I appreciate that when I was getting my divorce you

were sad but nonjudgmental. You didn't try to tell me what to do and you supported me in the best way you knew how.'

" 'I feel like we're getting to know one another not only as mother and daughter but as two open and caring people. You working with me on the "pets-on-wheels" project has been a special treat.'

" 'I'm fortunate that I was born and nurtured by you to be the happy, loving and successful person I am. I love you and hope that we can enjoy many more birthdays together.' "

When you become your own best parent and take responsibility for your own happiness, it becomes easier to feel good about and express your love for your parents. Recognizing how they have contributed to you allows you to better appreciate your interdependence with every other human being. We are all both parents and children. Making peace with your parents helps you to appreciate yourself and the uniqueness of your upbringing and family background.

The more you review and use the strategies and techniques contained in this book, the more you are likely to derive significant benefit. With a strong commitment to your personal transformation, you are likely to come face to face with your own desire to make the world a better place. The more you experience your personal power, the less you will feel helpless in confronting human problems. Your empathy expands for the suffering of others plagued by hunger, war, poverty and discrimination. No longer are you willing to see these as "someone else's problem" or matters to be solved exclusively by "experts." Taking charge of your life means freeing your own creative power to make a difference in the world. *Making peace with your parents is at the very core of the human experience: an adventure of the heart, to love and be loved. We must make peace with ourselves and our families if we are to make peace on Earth.*

References

Birren, James E., and R. Bruce Sloane, eds. *Handbook of Mental Health and Aging.* Englewood Cliffs, N.J.: Prentice-Hall, 1980.

Bloomfield, Harold H. *How to Enjoy the Love of Your Life: Over One Hundred Ways to Enrich Your Love Life.* New York: Doubleday, 1979.

————, and Robert B. Kory. *Inner Joy: New Strategies for Adding More Pleasure to Your Life.* New York: Wyden, 1980.

Bry, Adelaide, and Leonard Felder. *Learning to Love Forever: A Forty-Day Plan for a Love That Lasts.* New York: Macmillan, 1982.

Colgrove, Melba, Harold H. Bloomfield, and Peter McWilliams. *How to Survive the Loss of a Love.* New York: Bantam, 1977.

Halpern, Howard M. *Cutting Loose: A Guide to Adult Relationships with Your Parents.* New York: Simon & Schuster, 1977.

Hoffman, Bob. *No One Is to Blame: Getting a Loving Divorce from Mom and Dad.* Palo Alto, Calif.: Science and Behavior Books, 1979.

James, Muriel. *Breaking Free: Self-Reparenting for a New Life.* Reading, Mass.: Addison-Wesley, 1981.

Kübler-Ross, Elisabeth. *On Death and Dying.* New York: Macmillan, 1970.

Lazarus, Arnold A. *The Practice of Multimodal Therapy.* New York: McGraw-Hill, 1981.

Lieberman, Mendel, and Marion Hardie, *Resolving Family Conflicts: Everybody Wins.* Santa Cruz, Calif.: Unity Press, 1981.

Maslow, Abraham H., ed. *Motivation and Personality,* 2nd ed. New York: Harper and Row, 1970.

Missildine, W. Hugh. *Your Inner Child of the Past.* New York: Simon & Schuster, 1963.

Ray, Sondra. *I Deserve Love.* Millbrae, Calif.: Les Femmes, 1976.

Rogers, Carl R. *On Becoming a Person.* Boston: Houghton Mifflin, 1961.

Satir, Virginia M. *Conjoint Family Therapy,* revised ed. Palo Alto, Calif.: Science and Behavior Books, 1967.

Silverstone, Barbara, and Helen Kandel Hyman. *You and Your Aging Parent: The Modern Family's Guide to Emotional, Physical, and Financial Problems,* updated and expanded ed. New York: Pantheon, 1982.

Viscott, David. *Risking.* New York: Simon & Schuster, 1977.

About the Authors

HAROLD H. BLOOMFIELD, M.D., is a practicing psychiatrist and Director of Psychiatry, Psychotherapy and Health Training at the North County Holistic Health Center in Del Mar, California. He completed his psychiatric training at the Yale University School of Medicine, is a member of the American Psychiatric Association and is a founding member of the Association for Holistic Health and the American Holistic Medical Association. Dr. Bloomfield is a world-renowned lecturer and seminar leader. The books he has written or co-authored include *How to Survive the Loss of a Love; TM: Discovering Inner Energy and Overcoming Stress; The Holistic Way to Health and Happiness; How to Enjoy the Love of Your Life;* and *Inner Joy.*

LEONARD FELDER, PH.D., is a psychologist and writer who lives in Santa Monica, California. A graduate of Kenyon College, he has written for several magazines and held positions at Doubleday Publishing and American Express. He is the co-author of the book *Learning to Love Forever.*